In the Footsteps
of J. E. B. Stuart

Also by Clint Johnson

In the Footsteps of Stonewall Jackson
In the Footsteps of Robert E. Lee
Touring Virginia's and West Virginia's Civil War Sites
Touring the Carolinas' Civil War Sites
Civil War Blunders
Bull's-Eyes and Misfires

In the Footsteps
of J. E. B. Stuart

by
Clint Johnson

John F. Blair, Publisher   *Winston-Salem, North Carolina*

Published by John F. Blair, Publisher

_The paper in this book meets the guidelines
for permanence and durability of the
Committee on Production Guidelines for
Book Longevity of the Council on Library Resources._

Cover Images:

Painting:
c. 1900 by Henry Alexander Ogden
Courtesy of The Library of Congress, Prints & Photographs Division,
LC-USZC4-2462

Bottom row left to right:
St. Mary's Chapel, Fort Riley, Kansas;
Statue of Stuart in Richmond, Virginia;
Harpers Ferry, West Virginia

Library of Congress Cataloging-in-Publication Data

Johnson, Clint, 1953–
In the footsteps of J. E. B. Stuart / by Clint Johnson.
p.   cm.
Includes bibliographical references and index.
ISBN 0-89587-261-7 (alk. paper)
1.Stuart, Jeb, 1833–1864—Homes and haunts—Guidebooks.
2. Historic sites—United States—Guidebooks. I. Title
E467.1.S9J64 2003
973.7'42—dc21   2003011323

Design by Debra Long Hampton

Dedication

This book is dedicated to Barbara, my wife of nearly 20 years, who over our marriage has cheerfully acquiesced to visits to battlefields during our vacations, as long as she can stay in bed-and-breakfasts. She has put up with my travels away from her and my household duties while I've researched my books or refought the war as a reenactor. She has never been happy about the smells left behind in our vehicles by sweaty men wearing wool uniforms unchanged after several days, but she has never demanded that I drop my hobby. That is just one of the minor reasons I love her.

Map Index

Virginia
(See detailed map on page xx.)

West Virginia
1   Bunker Hill
2   Falling Waters
3   Harpers Ferry

Maryland
(See detailed map on page 106.)

Pennsylvania
4   Mercersburg
5   Chambersburg
6   Cashtown
7   Gettysburg
8   Hanover

New York
9   West Point

Michigan
10   Detroit

Kansas
11   Baldwin City
12   Fort Leavenworth
13   Fort Riley
14   Morland

Texas
15   Laredo

Contents

VIRGINIA

Northern Virginia

Central Virginia

Preface

Of all the ways to end one's life on earth, the death of Major General James Ewell Brown Stuart had to be among the most sad and ironic.

At one point in his life, he said that when it was his time to go, he hoped—and assumed—that it would be leading a cavalry charge. Several times during his last three years, he told close aides that he did not think he would survive the war.

Stuart didn't get his wish to die on the battlefield in defense of the South. His last moments were not spent on a war-horse with a saber in one hand and a pistol in the other. He died flat on his back in a bed, probably in his underwear. He was shot not through the heart, as heroes want to go, but through the intestines, a smelly, messy end to a remarkable and controversial life.

But even though we know Stuart died that way, we do not carry that image of him in our mind's eye. When Stuart's name is uttered, we think of a barrel-chested man in a crimson-lined cape sweeping his hat off his head and bowing low to admiring ladies—just before he steals a kiss from each one. We think of a man literally laughing at his enemies as he rides away from one close call after another, confident that he is a much better horseman than any enemy he will face. We think of a headquarters party where Mulatto Bob plays the bones and Sam Sweeney plays the banjo while 250-pound, six-foot-two Prussian soldier of fortune Heros von Borcke puts on a dress to imitate a farmer's daughter in a farcical play about invading Pennsylvania. At the center of the party is Stuart, laughing so hard he sheds tears. That is the picture many Southerners keep in their hearts.

Stuart stands at the center of the Confederate image. We think of J. E. B. as author Burke Davis titled him in a biography—*The Last Cavalier*. Stuart fit that dashing image. Though he was a deeply religious man who was dedicated to his wife, Flora, and his children, he loved flirting with the ladies. If given the choice to throw a party or attend a staff meeting, he always threw the party. If singing patriotic songs, he gravitated to those that mentioned him by name. If he saw a chance to play a practical joke on anyone— even a superior officer—he took it.

None of this detracts from the fact that Stuart was a careful tactician, a skilled scout, and a bold fighter.

True, Stuart had his weaknesses, the chief of which was sometimes forgetting his own importance to the army. His skills at scouting and raiding were critical to the early success of the Confederacy—as he liked to point out—yet he sometimes acted as if he were little more important than one of his cavalrymen. At the same time, he was always seeking approval from his superiors and his peers. When emptying his pockets after his death, aides found an order that addressed him like a corps commander and a lieutenant general—a role he filled only temporarily and a rank he never attained. The paper was nearly a year old, dating back to Chancellorsville in May 1863, when he took over the corps command of Stonewall Jackson after Jackson's wounding.

These seeming contradictions in Stuart's personality may explain why his reputation is still questioned today, particularly by those who criticize his absence from Robert E. Lee's close flanks in the early days of the Pennsylvania Campaign. Stuart's critics claim he ignored Lee's orders to screen the Confederate infantry from the soon-to-be-pursuing Army of the Potomac in favor of "riding a raid" for fun. By leaving Lee blind to what the Federals were doing, the critics say, Stuart shared in the blame for the Gettysburg defeat.

In reality, Stuart followed Lee's orders almost to the letter in terms of raiding close to Washington, disrupting communications, and securing supplies. But even in carrying out Lee's orders, Stuart still failed his commander. Stuart's major fault in the Pennsylvania Campaign was underestimating Lee's dependence on him. The facts now seem clear 140 years after Gettysburg. Stuart led the only cavalry Lee implicitly trusted. Had Stuart understood that, he would have almost certainly modified his raiding plans. Perhaps he would have ordered the two brigades he first assigned to Lee to switch out so he could lead the brigades closest to the commander. But what difference would this have made? Had Stuart arranged his brigades to satisfy Lee, there is no hard evidence that the Battle of Gettysburg would have ended differently, with the exception that Lee might have learned a bit sooner that the Federals were on his trail.

Stuart's complex nature colored what his admirers and detractors thought of him in his day. Some of his brigade commanders loved him. Others hated him. It is the same with history readers today. People think of Stuart as either a dandy or a military genius.

Of course, there's one thing on which everyone agrees: Stuart led a fascinating life. Fortunately, it was a life that can be traced with a little travel.

This book follows Stuart's life by visiting sites associated with him from his birth to his death. Stuart's career makes this somewhat difficult, since cavalrymen did not build forts, dig trenches, or stay in one place for long. Cavalrymen were in constant motion and so left behind little evidence of their passing. That means there is little to see at Stuart battlefields such as Solomon's Fork in Kansas and Brandy Station in Virginia, other than the lay of the land. Some places have been lost. All there is to see at Yellow Tavern, where Stuart was mortally wounded, are people mowing their lawns. All there is to see at the site in downtown Richmond where he died are rows of shabby office buildings and parking lots.

Still, there are plenty of sites where you can literally touch what Stuart touched. For example, you can handle the door knocker on the Lee home at Arlington National Cemetery. According to park rangers, it is the same knocker used by Stuart in 1859 to alert Robert E. Lee of John Brown's raid at Harpers Ferry. You can also walk into the reconstructed firehouse captured by Brown, where you can almost hear Stuart banging on the door and demanding the surrender of the insurgents. And you can visit the Virginia Historical Society in Richmond and gaze on the blood-soaked sash Stuart was wearing at Yellow Tavern. No one speaks when they first see this preserved artifact of "the Last Cavalier."

No, I have not attempted to include every single site where Stuart touched down at some point in his life. I think I have included most of the significant sites of his life, and those where something interesting happened.

Stuart's lasting spirit is expressed in the period song "Riding a Raid":

> Now each cavalier that loves honor and right,
> Let him follow the feather of Stuart tonight.
> Come tighten your girth and slacken your rein;
> Come buckle your blanket and holster again;
> Try the click of your trigger and balance your blade,
> For he must ride sure that goes riding a raid.

Acknowledgments

I thank Dr. Eugene Adcock of Winston-Salem, North Carolina, for helping track down some sites.

Joe Balicki, a historian in Fairfax County, Virginia, helped me find sites like Munson's Hill and Burke Station.

Debbie Bianchi aided me in locating historians in Fairfax County, Virginia.

Michael Boss of Hill City, Kansas, showed me the site of the sod fort where Stuart rested after his wounding at the Battle of Solomon's Fork.

Bill Boyd of Mount Airy, North Carolina, and the 26th Regiment North Carolina Troops Reactivated is a favorite traveling buddy who navigates the back roads for me while I drive.

Charles Bush, a student at Western Carolina University and a fellow reenactor in the 26th North Carolina, helped me find some sites in Pennsylvania, Maryland, and Virginia.

Patricia Spurrier Bright of the United States Cavalry Association and Research Library at Fort Riley, Kansas, established which buildings existed during Stuart's posting there.

James R. Droegemeyer helped me find the location of The Bower and loaned me photos of this Stuart headquarters.

Robert Durham loaned me his manuscript on the Battle of Solomon's Fork, Kansas.

Joe Ferrell of St. Albans, West Virginia, loaned me photographs of the graves of Union general Phillip St. George Cooke, Union general David M. Gregg, and Confederate general Beverly Robertson.

Kay Hawks, secretary of the Norton County (Kansas) Historical Society and Museum, helped me track down the site of Stuart's wounding in his Cheyenne skirmish.

Sheriff Don Scot of Graham County, Kansas, helped me photograph the site.

Cheryl Knaut at Hollywood Cemetery in Richmond helped me find the grave of Channing Price, one of Stuart's aides.

William McKale, acting director of the United States Cavalry Museum at Fort Riley, helped me establish which buildings existed during Stuart's posting and sent me an electronic version of the Fort Riley driving tour.

Dick Moore, public-relations director for Emory & Henry College, and John Herbert Roper, a history professor at the college, informed me about which buildings existed while Stuart was a student there.

James Perry, historian for the Chesapeake & Ohio Canal National Historical Park, and Kathy Sholl, public-affairs assistant at the park, helped me find Rowser's Ford.

Tom Perry of Mount Airy, North Carolina, president of the J. E. B. Stuart Historic Preservation Trust, provided invaluable help in assembling a list of Stuart sites and in granting me a look at his exhaustive research on where Stuart served before the war. He also merits special mention for his dedication to preserving Stuart's birthplace.

Donna Seifert, a historian in Fairfax County, Virginia, helped me find Stuart's headquarters there.

Larry Z. Daily of Shepherdstown, West Virginia, allowed me the use of his photo of Beaver Dam Station, Virginia.

Donald Pfanz, historian at Chancellorsville National Battlefield Park, allowed me the use of his photo of Hazel Grove.

My thanks also go to the staff of the Forsyth County (North Carolina) Public Library, for helping me track down old books through interlibrary loan.

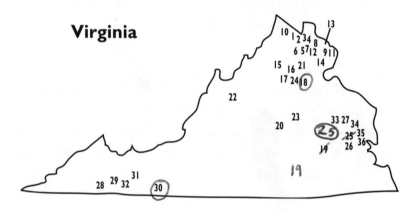

Virginia

1	Upperville	20	Rochelle
2	Atoka	21	Kelly's Ford
3	Middleburg	22	Staunton
4	Aldie	23	Verdiersville
5	Auburn	24	Warrenton
6	Buckland Mills	25	Richmond
7	Catlett's Station	26	Evelynton Heights &
8	Dranesville		Berkeley Plantation
9	Fairfax	27	Yellow Tavern
10	Berryville	28	Abingdon
11	Arlington	29	Emory
12	Manassas National Battlefield	30	Laurel Hill
13	Falls Church	31	Saltville
14	Qui Vive	32	Glade Spring
15	Amissville	33	Beaver Dam Station
16	Brandy Station	34	Ashland
17	Cedar Mountain	35	Studley
18	Chancellorsville	36	Old Church Tavern
19	Blackstone		

⊗ birth pl.

⊗

Stuart delivered a note to Lee at Arlington House that sent Lee to capture John Brown at Harpers Ferry.

Northern Virginia

Arlington

> *Arlington is the name of a county, a city, a National Cemetery, a plantation, and a famous home. The city is located across the Memorial Bridge from Washington, D.C. Arlington National Cemetery is accessible off the George Washington Parkway. The Lee-Custis mansion is at the top of the largest hill in the cemetery. Call 703-695-3250 for information.*

It was to Arlington, the Lee-Custis mansion, that United States Army lieutenant J. E. B. Stuart delivered a note to United States Army lieutenant colonel Robert E. Lee on October 17, 1859.

Stuart had been hanging around the War Department offices in

Washington waiting to discuss his invention of a hook that would transfer a cavalryman's saber from his belt to his horse's saddle. While he was waiting to pitch his invention, a frantic telegram arrived from the president of the Baltimore & Ohio Railroad, who said that trains were being stopped from passing through Harpers Ferry by strangers who were trying to launch a slave insurrection. Secretary of War John Floyd dashed off a note to Lee and handed it to Stuart, who had attended West Point during Lee's term as superintendent. Stuart rushed to Arlington, found Lee at home, and brought him back to the War Department.

That evening, Stuart volunteered to accompany Lee to Harpers Ferry as his aide. It would be the first of many times he would serve Lee.

Arlington was built by Mary Custis Lee's father, who was the step-grandson of George Washington. Early in 1861, it was confiscated by the Federal government. In 1864, its grounds were converted into the National Cemetery.

According to park rangers at Arlington, Stuart used the knocker now on the door. During the Civil War, the knocker was among the household inventory stolen by occupying Union soldiers. In the early 1990s, a descendant of the thieving soldier returned the knocker to Arlington, where it was remounted.

Falls Church

Falls Church, a suburb about 12 miles west of Washington, D.C., is easily accessed via I-66, US 50, or US 29. A portion of Munson's Hill is now a city park in Falls Church. The park is located at 6027 Munson Hill Road. From VA 7 less than a mile south of its intersection with US 50, turn onto Glenmore Drive. Drive one block and turn left onto Munson Hill Road. Watch for the two-acre park on the left.

The residential area around Munson's, Mason's, and Upton's Hills looks very different today from the way it appeared in 1861, when it was undeveloped, little-forested land from which Stuart could see Washington. Today, the swing sets of a city park stand in the general area where Stuart maintained a tent headquarters in August and September 1861 in anticipation of attacking Washington.

This could have been a historically significant location. Had the Confederacy wanted to attack Washington that summer, it would have launched its assault from this playground. Today, you'll find no historical marker noting this as Stuart's former headquarters, though there is a J. E. B. Stuart High School nearby.

On July 21, 1861, the day the Federals fled in panic after First Manassas, General Thomas J. Jackson, now sporting the new nickname "Stonewall," strongly urged pursuit into Washington itself. President Jefferson Davis, who had ridden to the front lines, considered the idea but finally decided against an immediate attack, persuaded that the Confederate army was as disorganized in victory as the Federal army was in defeat.

Colonel Stuart, attached to Jackson's command, secured permission to follow the Federals to the outskirts of Washington. He set up camp here at Munson's Hill to keep watch on Union activity in the city and to prepare for what he expected would be an all-out attack before the summer was done.

Life at Munson's Hill must have been tense. Stuart maintained a string of picket posts from here to the Potomac River, then back to Confederate headquarters near Manassas. Some men wrote letters home describing how Stuart often rode among the posts, spending more time in the saddle than they would have expected for a commander. The accommodations were Spartan. One man wrote that Stuart would flop down to sleep at Munson's Hill without even throwing a blanket over himself.

On September 12, General James Longstreet wrote the following dispatch: "[Stuart] has been most untiring in the discharge of his duties at . . . advanced positions, after having driven the enemy from Mason's, Munson's, and Upton's Hills. In these and other less important skirmishes he has been entirely successful. Where he has lost a man, he has brought in at least two of the enemy, dead or alive. Colonel Stuart has, I think, fairly won his claim to brigadier, and I hope the commanding generals will unite with me in recommending him for that promotion."

Within a few days, Stuart would learn he had been promoted to brigadier general for his service at Manassas and his scouting duties here at Munson's Hill.

Even the Confederate infantrymen discovered they were fond of Stuart, though liking any cavalryman is odd for a foot soldier. Writing in the *Southern Historical Papers* after the war, J. William Jones, a member of the 13th Virginia Regiment, described his experience at Munson's Hill:

It was my privilege to see a good deal of Stuart at this period, at his head-quarters, on a red blanket, spread under a pine tree on Munson's hill. His athletic frame indicating that he was a splendid war machine—his lofty forehead, flashing blue eyes, prominent nose, heavy, reddish-brown whiskers and mustache—his beaming countenance and clear, ringing laughter, and his prompt decision, rapid execution and gallant dash, all showed that he was a born leader of men, and pointed him out as a model cavalryman. Those were merry days on the outpost, when we fought for a peach orchard, a tomato patch, or a cornfield, when Stuart would call for volunteers to drive in the enemy's pickets, or amuse himself with having Rosser's artillery "practice" at Professor Lowe's balloon, or sending up a kite with lantern attached, or causing the long roll to beat along McClellan's whole front, by sending up sky-rockets at night from different points.

Another joke Stuart played on McClellan at Munson's Hill was the mounting of "Quaker guns"—large trees stripped of their limbs and painted black. From a distance, they looked like cannons poking through the earthworks Stuart had constructed around the hill. McClellan used the sightings of these "cannons" to prove that the South would be no pushover. Whether Stuart invented the Quaker gun or was following orders from headquarters is unknown, but it is clear that the black tree trunks frightened the Federal army and kept it immobile for months.

The Confederate government, to Stuart's dismay, never tried to launch a major attack from this outpost. Instead, it decided to let the Federals make the next move, just as it had waited for the attack at Manassas. After lingering here for weeks, Stuart was finally ordered back deeper into Virginia. He would not see Munson's Hill again. Indeed, the hill was not used again by Confederate troops, though it was frequently visited by Union soldiers throughout the war.

Dranesville

The Dranesville Tavern is located in a public park operated by Fairfax County. The park is outside Dranesville at 11919 Leesburg Turnpike (VA 7), just east of the intersection with Fairfax County Parkway.

Stuart was famously criticized in the summer of 1863 for poor judgment in not keeping track of Federal forces. But he first displayed that trait a year and a half earlier.

After the Union defeat at nearby Balls Bluff in November 1861, both sides were still feeling each other out in northern Virginia. On December 20, the opposing forces decided to forage in the same area. Stuart, in command of 150 cavalrymen and more than 1,500 infantrymen, did not send out a reconnoitering patrol before his cavalrymen ran into nearly 4,000 Federals near Dranesville Tavern. Frantic that the foragers and their wagons were exposed to capture, Stuart hastily arranged a defense along the road, but the Federals, already set up on higher ground, fired into the Confederates, who were forced into the open road by the dense undergrowth alongside it. After about two hours of fighting, Stuart had to retreat. His losses were heavy: 43 dead, compared to just seven for

Dranesville Tavern

the Federals. Some Confederates were killed by friendly fire, as at least two Southern regiments fired into each other by mistake.

While the action at Dranesville was tiny compared to First Manassas and the larger battles soon to come, it did have a huge effect on Northern morale. In June, the Union had lost at Big Bethel on the Virginia Peninsula but won at Rich Mountain. In July, it lost at First Manassas. In August, it captured Confederate forts along the Outer Banks of North Carolina, but that victory was clouded just three months later by the disaster at Balls Bluff. Now, the North finally had a victory on the soil of northern Virginia, almost within sight of Washington. It was played up in the Northern newspapers as a larger event than it really was.

Stuart shrugged off the loss at Dranesville Tavern, even claiming in his report that the battle was a success, in that the Federals had not captured his wagon train. In reality, Stuart had simply not scouted the Leesburg Turnpike, a basic mistake he should not have been making six months into the war. Had the Confederate army been more organized at the time, it is conceivable that Stuart might have been called to account for his scouting failures, but nothing seems to have been done.

Fairfax/Burke/Qui Vive

The original Fairfax Court House is at the intersection of Chain Bridge Road (VA 123) and US 50 about 10 miles west of Arlington. Antonia Ford's house is the brick building at 3977 Chain Bridge Road. Though the home now serves as office space, there is a display in the lobby about Antonia's life.

The village of Burke lies a short distance south of Fairfax. The former site of Qui Vive, the fun-loving Stuart's headquarters, is just west of Fairfax.

Stuart enjoyed having his wife, Flora, near him. When he was ordered to keep a lookout post at Munson's Hill, he found accommodations for her in a house in Fairfax Court House.

That house was probably the home of 23-year-old Antonia Ford, daughter of a prominent businessman. Stuart visited here often and became friends with Antonia. He even went so far as to give her a commission in the Confederate army. It read, "Know ye: that reposing special confidence in the patriotism, fidelity and ability of Miss Antonia Ford, I, James E. B. Stuart, by virtue of the power vested in me as a brigadier general in the Provisional Army of the Confederate States of America, do hereby appoint and commission her my honorary aide-de-camp. She will be obeyed, respected and admired by all the lovers of a noble nature."

The commission was a joke, a party favor bearing the autograph of a popular general. It was given to Antonia in thanks for her hospitality. But the joke soon turned sour.

On the evening of March 9, 1863, Confederate captain John

The home of Antonia Ford

Singleton Mosby and his men rode into Fairfax Court House, kidnapped Union general Edward Stoughton and several other officers, and stole more than 50 horses. The following morning, an embarrassed Union army swooped down upon the town. Federal officials all the way up to Secretary of War Edwin Stanton were desperate to find some explanation as to how a handful of Confederates had ridden more than 50 miles behind Union lines to pull off such a successful raid. Every home in Fairfax Court House was invaded and searched for evidence of spying.

That evidence was discovered at the Ford home. Though the language indicated that the "commission" was a joke meant to compliment Antonia on her beauty, she was arrested for spying and sent to the notorious Capitol Prison in Washington, the same place where Rose O'Neal Greenhow, the real Southern spy who had warned the Confederacy about plans for Manassas, had been kept.

Antonia's beauty captivated the officer who arrested her, Major Joseph Willard, owner of the prominent Willard Hotel in downtown Washington. Every chance he got, he visited her in prison. He worked for her release. When that was accomplished in 1864,

he married her. Antonia had a sense of humor about her imprison-
ment. She reportedly said, "I knew I could not revenge myself on
the whole nation, but felt very capable of tormenting one Yankee
to death, so I took the major." She bore three children but died at
age 33 in 1871, apparently from an immune system weakened by
the year she spent in the cold, damp prison.

While rumors persist that Antonia was a spy for Stuart and
Mosby, no records survive of any such work. Mosby said he met
Antonia once but never used her for spying. He wrote, "She was as
innocent of spying as Mr. Lincoln." It appears that Antonia's only
real crime was seeking Stuart's autograph.

To take a short side trip, drive south on Chain Bridge Road
(VA 123) for 3.3 miles to Fairfax Station Road (VA 660). It was
near this intersection that Stuart was resting and grazing his horse
on June 27, 1863, on his way to cross the Potomac when a Union
patrol discovered him. He leaped upon his mount without rein-
serting the horse's bit. Using only voice commands and leg pres-
sure to urge the horse onward, and holding onto its mane and hal-
ter, Stuart was able to outdistance his pursuers as he ran toward
his main body of troops. As soon as the Federals saw the thousands
of troopers, they broke off their chase.

Stuart was pestered by such raids by Federal cavalry all the
way to Gettysburg. While Lee's infantry was able to march into
Pennsylvania virtually unmolested until it engaged in the major
battle, Stuart's cavalry seems to have been attacked before it even
left Virginia.

A couple of other Stuart sites are located near Fairfax, though
there is little to see at either one today.

The village of Burke, formerly called Burke's Station, lies two
miles south at the intersection of CR 651 and CR 652. After attacking a Federal column south of what is now Occoquan in De-

cember 1862, Stuart pressed northward to Burke's Station. An advance party was able to capture the telegraph operator before he could get off a warning to Washington. Stuart then had his own telegraph operator monitor the messages Burke Station received about Stuart's whereabouts. The new operator also transmitted false messages. Finally, Stuart sent a message to Union quartermaster general Montgomery Meigs complaining that poor-quality Union mules made moving captured Union wagons difficult. Stuart left Burke's Station without waiting for a reply.

Stuart's farmhouse headquarters for the winter of 1861-62 was located north of the intersection of US 29 and West Ox Road (CR 608) just west of Fairfax. It was called Qui Vive—or "Who Goes There?"—after the French picket challenge. The house was abandoned by the Millan family and has long since disappeared under urban development.

It was at Qui Vive that Stuart began to groom his reputation for keeping a fun-loving camp. Any first-time visitor knew instantly that this was not a typical general's compound. First of all, there was a Blakely cannon near the house, unusual since it was imported from England. Underneath the cannon was a giant raccoon that snapped at anyone who tried to get close enough to inspect the cannon. Stuart would roar with laughter whenever this happened.

On his first visit to Qui Vive, John Esten Cooke, the cousin of Stuart's wife, noted that Stuart wore a plume in his hat and dressed in a fine gray uniform. Cooke was introduced to two Northern women who had been caught trying to get through to the Federal lines in Alexandria. Stuart asked several black musicians and dancers to entertain them while he worked at his desk. The banjo and guitar playing, accompanied by bird calls given by one of the musicians, soon attracted men from all over the camp, who crowded the doors and windows to watch the fun. When Stuart asked the women if they had enjoyed the show, one replied, "You Rebels do seem to enjoy yourselves!" As the two women, apparently grandmother and granddaughter, left the next day to be escorted to the Federal lines, Stuart kissed the hand of the teenager but not that of the older woman. When asked why, he replied, "The old lady's hand had a glove on it!" He then roared with laughter.

In winter quarters, Stuart had time to put together his staff. It was here that he met Private John Singleton Mosby, who would become his most trusted scout and eventually end up the most famous colonel in either army. And it was here that Major John Pelham was given command of Stuart's horse artillery. Colonel Fitzhugh Lee, nephew of Robert E. Lee, became one of Stuart's closest friends and most trusted brigade commanders here.

It was also at Qui Vive that Stuart began to keep his short but firm list of enemies. Heading that list was his father-in-law, General Phillip St. George Cooke, who had stayed in the Union. Stuart changed his son's name from Phillip to Jimmy so there would be nothing to remind him of Cooke. And Stuart was at Qui Vive when he decided that he didn't like Confederate colonel (later general) Beverly H. Robertson, calling him "the most troublesome man I have ever met." Stuart's assessment may have been based on the fact that Robertson was a prewar friend of General Cooke's. Robertson did not join the Confederate army until after First Manassas in July 1861, which also made Stuart suspicious of him.

Once March 1862 rolled around, Stuart abandoned Qui Vive for the saddle, where he felt most at home.

Manassas National Battlefield/
Warrenton/Amissville

Manassas National Battlefield is about 20 miles west of Washington. From I-66, drive north on VA 234 (Sudley Road) to the park entrance.

Stuart saw action at both First Manassas in July 1861 and Second Manassas in August 1862. To see where he fought at First Manassas, walk back toward the Sudley Road entrance from the parking lot at the visitor center. About 20 feet inside the park along the tree line is a depression with the faint outline of a road leading toward I-66. This was the original Sudley Road, on which Stuart and his First Virginia Regiment, or Black Horse Cavalry, won their fame. To see where he fought at Second Manassas, leave the visitor center, turn right on Sudley Road, drive to the traffic light, and turn left on US 29. Proceed to the edge of the park and turn left into the parking lot for Lee Hill. Here is where Second Manassas began, at a spot believed to be Lee's headquarters. It was west of here along what is now US 29 that Stuart created a ruse that frightened the Federals.

The park is open every day of the week. A small admission fee is charged. Call 703-361-1339 for more information.

Warrenton and Amissville lie southwest of Manassas along US 211.

In the spring and early summer of 1861, politicians in both the North and the South believed that one large battle could settle the war. The Confederates correctly figured that Manassas Junction would be a key Union target. If the Federals could capture Manassas, they could get a toehold in the South for shipping supplies to distant armies.

On the morning of July 21, Colonel Stuart and two companies of his First Virginia Cavalry were in the roadbed at Sudley Road waiting impatiently for someone—anyone—to give them orders. To the north, the Federals had already crossed Sudley Ford and Matthews Hill and were now advancing on Henry House Hill, just out of sight but not out of earshot.

Stuart knew that his men, probably numbering fewer than 200, could make little difference in the raging battle he could not see. Judging from the sound of the gunfire, the Federals were advancing with thousands of infantry and dozens of cannons. His men were armed only with Colt and Remington pistols, carbines, a smattering of shotguns, and sabers.

At around two that afternoon, at least six hours after the battle had opened, Stuart got his orders, vague as they were. He was told to simply advance on the field and rush to where the shooting was the hottest.

As Stuart's men, nicknamed the Black Horse Cavalry for obvi-

Henry House

ous reasons, trotted onto the field, Stuart spied what he thought was the First Louisiana Special Battalion, a unit destined to become known as the Louisiana Tigers. The Tigers were a Zouave unit who dressed in colorful red, white, blue, and tan uniforms patterned after French Moroccan soldiers. As Stuart drew close, it appeared to him that the Louisianans were afraid of his men. He called to them, "Don't run, boys! We are here!"

More of the Zouaves began to turn away. It was then that Stuart noticed the flag they were carrying. It was the United States flag. These Zouaves were not from Louisiana, but rather from New York City. They were the 11th New York Regiment, also known as the New York Fire Zouaves, made up of firemen from the boroughs of New York.

No doubt chuckling to himself over his mistake, Stuart ordered his cavalrymen to draw their sabers. They then closed on the Zouaves from a distance that could not have been more than 100 yards. The Zouaves were able to get off one volley, killing at least nine men before the Virginians were among them, slashing their sabers with one hand and firing pistols with the other while controlling their horses with their knees. The Zouaves soon fled in panic. The skirmish was over within minutes.

What Stuart did not know was that the New York Fire Zouaves had been sent forward to support a battery of Union artillery that was forming on General Thomas Jackson's left flank. Had the New York infantry reached those guns and had time to set up a defense before Stuart arrived, it might have turned the tide of battle. Stuart's timely charge kept the Federals on that flank in turmoil.

Stuart and his men fought for another two hours, mostly directing the artillery fire of a battery he appropriated and sending messages to the infantry from his relatively smoke-free vantage point. His messages to the brigade of General Jubal Early helped

Early pour fire into the Federal flank. Later, Early commented in a written report, "Stuart did as much in saving the battle of First Manassas as any subordinate officer who participated in it, and yet he has never received any credit for it, in the official reports or otherwise. His own report is very brief and incomplete."

Stuart stayed mostly on Sudley Road, finally ending up near Sudley Ford, where he set up a makeshift headquarters as his men chased the Federals back toward Washington. He would stay at this headquarters only two days before moving to Fairfax Court House and then Munson's Hill, the closest he or any other Confederate would advance on Washington from Virginia during the war.

After the battle, Stuart wrote his wife a letter predicting that he would likely be made a general for his service at Manassas. Already showing the cleverness for which he would become known, he modestly claimed little credit in his own report, knowing that the officers he had helped, such as Early, would speak highly of him in their reports.

Like his friend Jackson, Stuart would return to the scene of his first big battle 13 months later. And much as Jackson had played a major role in saving the day for the Confederates at First Manassas, Stuart would play a major role in saving Jackson at Second Manassas.

Second Manassas was a battle Lee planned after digesting the intelligence Stuart brought him from the raid at Catlett's Station. Knowing that he had to hurt Union general John Pope before McClellan joined him, Lee sent Jackson and Stuart from Culpeper on a rapid march around Pope's flank and toward his rear at Bristoe Station and Manassas Junction.

Pope took the bait, reversing his direction and marching toward Manassas with his entire army. Having sent only half his army—Jackson's corps—Lee was thus able to dispatch an undetected Longstreet in pursuit of Pope. With luck and good planning,

Pope would be caught in a vise with Jackson on one side and Longstreet on the other.

Stuart's men were among the first to arrive at Manassas Junction, about eight miles from the battlefield of July 1861. There, they surprised Federals who were stockpiling food. Stuart held the town until Jackson's infantry arrived to start divvying up the supplies among the infantrymen. Some of those Southerners must have wondered about their ability to defeat a Yankee nation that could ship canned oysters to its men in the field.

After leaving downtown Manassas Junction, Jackson deployed his men in what has since become known as the Unfinished Railroad Cut, located to the northwest. Hunkered down in trenches behind a railroad embankment and the tree line, his entire corps was almost invisible. Pope's advance forces never knew what hit them when Jackson's men rushed out to pound them on August 29, 1862, then retreated back into their railroad cut to await the bulk of Pope's army.

Stuart had little part in the fighting, riding back and

The original Sudley Road where Stuart's troops waited to ambush the Federals at First Manassas

forth between Jackson and the advancing column of Longstreet to make sure Jackson wouldn't have to face Pope on his own.

On what is now the west side of Manassas National Battlefield along US 29, General Beverly Robertson, one of Stuart's least-liked and least-dependable brigadiers, came up a winner. He reported to Stuart that he had spotted a large body of Federal infantry. A concerned Stuart rode ahead and was dismayed at what he saw: a Union corps. The advance elements of McClellan's army had arrived. The corps belonged to General Fitz John Porter, the same capable soldier who had beaten Lee at Beaver Dam Creek, Gaines Mill, and Malvern Hill during the Seven Days' Campaign. If Porter successfully linked with Pope, Jackson would be in trouble, Stuart knew. The major problem was that Longstreet's corps was not yet in place on Jackson's flank.

Stuart then employed an ancient trick that had fooled opposing generals for centuries. He had his men drag tree branches behind their horses down what is now US 29, creating clouds of dust that Porter interpreted as massive numbers of infantry arriving on the battlefield. Ordered by Pope to attack Jackson immediately, Porter refused. Having just arrived on the battlefield, he demanded the chance to do his own scouting.

Stuart's trick of dragging the branches made Porter believe Longstreet had already arrived, when he was actually still marching toward the action. But Pope, the commanding Union general on the field, had not seen Stuart's dust cloud. He refused to believe that the Confederates he knew to be hiding in the Unfinished Railroad Cut (Jackson's men) were being reinforced by more troops (Longstreet's men). While Pope and Porter argued over Porter's refusal to attack, Longstreet filed, unseen, into place beside Jackson.

On the next day, August 30, a reluctant Porter finally agreed to Pope's demand that he attack Jackson's lines. Longstreet's men came pouring out of their trenches and fell onto Porter's flank, which resulted in the near rout of Pope's entire army. Only a determined Union defense near where Jackson and Stuart had first won fame on Henry House Hill during First Manassas saved Pope's army from destruction.

It is Longstreet's flank attack on August 30 that is generally credited with winning Second Manassas, but it was the August 29 ruse by Stuart that allowed Longstreet time to file into the trenches. Lee congratulated Stuart for "performing most important and valuable service."

In June, Stuart had ridden around McClellan. In mid-August, he had ruined Lee's chance at destroying Pope by losing an order. One week later, he captured Pope's dispatch book. Now, a week after that, he fooled an entire Union corps with a dust cloud. Stuart was at the top of his game.

If you care to make a brief side trip to visit the graves of a couple of Stuart associates, follow US 29 southwest from Manassas. It is about 20 miles to the town of Warrenton. Warrenton City Cemetery is located at the intersection of Main and Pelham Streets.

Look to the right of the Confederate statue to see the surprisingly modest tombstone of Colonel John Singleton Mosby. Mosby started the war as a private, proved his worth as a scout, and then slowly but surely convinced the Confederate high command of the value of partisan rangers operating in the rear of Union lines. Never in command of more than a few hundred men at any one time, Mosby tied up thousands of Union soldiers, who chased him all over northern Virginia without ever running him to ground. He successfully scouted Stuart's Ride Around McClellan and Stuart's crossing of the Potomac to launch the Pennsylvania Campaign.

From Mosby's grave, follow the paved road to the right. Look for what appears to be a square wall of boxwood plants. Inside is

*Gravesite of John Singleton
Mosby in the Warrenton City
Cemetery*

*Gravesite of Lundsford Lindsay
Lomax in the Warrenton City
Cemetery*

the grave of General Lundsford Lindsay Lomax. Lomax would never
have served in the war had it not been for Stuart. In 1857 in frontier Kansas, Lomax was facing an armed Indian when Stuart saved
his life with a saber slash that severely wounded the Indian. His
attention now directed at Stuart, the Indian fired the pistol shot he
had intended for Lomax into Stuart's chest. Both of the lieuten-
ants—but not the Cheyenne—survived the Indian wars. Historians
are thankful for Lomax's return to health. He went on to become
the primary editor of the *Official Records of the War of the Rebellion*,
the 128 volumes of orders and reports that are still the primary
source of information on the war. He also served as commissioner
of Gettysburg National Battlefield Park from 1905 to 1913.

It is worth noting that Stuart had a close call—and suffered a
blow that would change his grooming habits—at the village of
Amissville, located on US 211 about 10 miles southwest of
Warrenton.

On November 10, 1862, Stuart was dealing with harassment by Federal patrols near Amissville. That day, the Federals were doing a better than average job of pushing back against Stuart, thanks to the artillery they had in their support. Stuart's men were falling back when he ordered some sharpshooters to line up to hit the pursuing Federals. In an apparent attempt to offer himself as a lure, he ventured out of the tree line in full view of the advancing enemy. Aide Heros von Borcke yelled that Stuart was not where he should be. Stuart yelled in answer that if von Borcke was frightened, he could depart the field. Unwilling to leave his general in harm's way but feeling the heat of the enemy, von Borcke stepped behind a tree, which was hit by three bullets just seconds later. That got Stuart's attention. He finally turned to melt into the woods, but before he did, a Federal Minie ball took off half his mustache.

That night, an amused von Borcke told General Lee about Stuart's close call. Some photos of Stuart taken during the war years show a carefully cared-for, flamboyant mustache stretching to the sides of his face. Other photos show the mustache drooping and disappearing in a bushy beard. Perhaps Stuart changed his look to hide his missing mustache.

One has to wonder if there was a personal issue behind Stuart's flamboyant bravery in the face of an advancing enemy. Just a week earlier, he had learned from a telegram from his wife, Flora, that their daughter, also named Flora, had died of fever. When he received the telegram, Stuart collapsed in tears. He remarked to staff members that he would never get over his daughter's death.

Earlier, he had told his wife that pressing command duties would not allow him to visit their ill daughter.

There is nothing in Amissville to commemorate Stuart's close call.

Catlett's Station as it appears today

Catlett's Station

Catlett's Station is located at the intersection of VA 28 and Elk Run Road about 15 miles southwest of Manassas. Look for a Virginia Trails sign at the corner of Elk Run Road and Old Catlett Road; the sign explains the engagement that took place here.

On August 17, 1862, Stuart aide Norman Fitzhugh was captured at Verdiersville with a copy of the cavalry's orders to sweep behind Union general John Pope to trap his army between the Rappahannock and the Rapidan Rivers. The Confederates had to cancel that plan to crush Pope. Lee was now anxious to find some other way to attack Pope's force before the army of George McClellan could link with it.

Stuart proposed that he lead a raid in the same general direction he would have taken if the orders hadn't been captured. He specifically targeted Catlett's Station, where he would burn the bridge of the Orange & Alexandria Railroad, which spanned Cedar

Run just north of this station. By destroying Pope's ability to bring in supplies, Stuart hoped he could at least slow down any attempt to reinforce his army. Lee, likely still irritated that Stuart had indirectly spoiled his perfect plan by allowing his aide to be captured with the secret orders, readily agreed.

On August 22, Stuart started with 1,500 men from Orange Court House. Along the way, he stopped in Warrenton to see what intelligence he might get from the citizens of the occupied town. A young woman told him that if he ran into a certain Union officer at Catlett's Station, Stuart should capture him and send him immediately to Richmond. The officer had flirtatiously bet the woman a bottle of wine that he would be in Richmond in 30 days. The young woman told Stuart she would happily pay off the bet if Stuart found him. Stuart, always ready to oblige a pretty female, took down the officer's name.

As night came, so did a violent thunderstorm that hampered Stuart's men's ability to see where they were going. By lucky chance, they stumbled across a black laborer who claimed to know Stuart. He offered to lead the force into Catlett's Station and to point out where the troopers might meet resistance.

With the help of the laborer, whose information proved true, Stuart's men swept into Catlett's Station and captured the entire camp. Much to their surprise, it turned out to be the headquarters camp of Pope himself, though the commanding general was in Washington at that time. Stuart did capture Pope's dress uniform and more than a half-million dollars sent to the camp for the September payroll. While searching a tent, one of Stuart's aides reached for a buffalo robe to take as a souvenir, only to back off when the huge Newfoundland hound lying on it gave a warning growl. The aide refused to kill the loyal dog to get the robe.

But the objective of the raid—destroying the railroad bridge over Cedar Run—was not accomplished. Curiously, two different officers on Stuart's staff who later wrote biographies of him gave two different explanations. Major Henry McClellan said the timbers were too wet and that Stuart's men didn't have axes that would cut them. Lieutenant Colonel W. W. Blackford said that the Federal infantry guarding the bridge was too strong to attack. What neither writer explained was why the two artillery pieces Stuart carried on the raid were not used to blast the timbers into splinters. The Confederates might have at least weakened the timbers by canister fire, opening the possibility that a Federal locomotive might collapse the bridge and make repairs much more difficult.

Stuart found two interesting prisoners among the lot he captured. One was the Union officer who had bragged he would be in Richmond within the month; Stuart told him he would be stopping in Warrenton to pick up his bottle of wine before being taken to Libby Prison. The other was a woman posing as a male soldier. She asked Stuart to let her go because of her gender. Stuart answered that if she had joined the army to fight as a man, she should be willing to experience prison as a man, too. He refused her request.

On its face, the Catlett's Station raid was both a success and a failure. Stuart had ridden behind enemy lines with few losses and had captured the camp of the opposing commanding general. Already a media star for his Ride Around McClellan in June, Stuart followed that with his Ride into Pope's headquarters in August. The newspapers ate it up. They had a father figure in Lee and now a merry raider son in Stuart. On the other hand, the railroad bridge had not been burned. And many of the prisoners Stuart captured got away in the darkness and confusion. The supplies that were captured were headquarters luxuries rather than arms, ammunition, and food that could be used by Lee's infantry.

Among the loot captured from Pope's tent was his dispatch

book, which detailed his past orders. While certainly not an even trade for the secret orders Pope had captured from Stuart's aide, the dispatches revealed quite a bit about the Union army that Lee found useful. Most important were the repeated mentions of his strength—45,000 men—a figure Lee had not previously known. The book also confirmed what Lee had suspected: Pope intended to wait until McClellan reached him before launching an offensive against the Army of Northern Virginia. Lee determined to use that information to make his own first move. He forgave Stuart for not burning the bridge.

Delighted that he had Pope's coat, Stuart wrote the Federal general a note offering to trade it for Stuart's captured plumed hat, of which he had grown fond, though he'd only owned it a few days. A fuming Pope did not answer the polite note. Pope's coat went on display in Richmond. Newspapers described it in detail, and hundreds of curious civilians went to see it as if it were a museum object.

Just as Stuart's Ride Around McClellan led to the Seven Days' Campaign, his Catlett's Station raid led to Second Manassas.

Auburn

Auburn is a small village located about five miles west of Catlett's Station and about 20 miles southwest of Manassas. It lies on CR 667 (Lower Dumfries Road), which may be reached via VA 28 at Catlett's Station. Look for the historical marker commemorating the battle at Auburn. Just north of the marker is a little valley visible from the road that seems to fit the description of Stuart's hiding place.

*The sunken valley near Auburn where Stuart
hid his force in October 1864*

On October 12, 1863, Stuart, three brigades of cavalry, and
seven cannons were on their way to Catlett's Station for a scouting
mission when they ran into the rear guard of the Federal infantry
marching north. Before Stuart could attack, he discovered two more
Union corps closing up on the first. There was one problem: He
was in the middle between the two columns. He had literally
stumbled into the middle of the Army of the Potomac.

Greatly outnumbered, Stuart did something that was rare for
him: He declined to fight. Instead, he found a sunken valley at
Auburn that was large enough to hide his entire force, which likely
numbered around 2,000 men. He moved the men and horses into
the valley, which was virtually next to the road, and issued whis-
pered orders for everyone to keep themselves and their horses and
mules quiet. During the night, he sent couriers out at six different
times to Lee asking for infantry relief.

Though separated from the Confederates by no more than 150
yards, the tired, marching Yankees apparently heard nothing.

At dawn, Lee's infantry came to the rescue, opening volleys
from the west. While the surprised Federals were forming, Stuart's
men pushed their cannons to the crest of a ridge. Attacked on both

sides, the thoroughly confused Federals allowed Stuart's men to push through them to safety.

It was from Auburn that Stuart advanced from a real trap into a false trap of his own making at Buckland Mills just a few days later.

Buckland Mills

Broad Run, where the Buckland Races started, is about 8.5 miles north of Warrenton on US 15/US 29 North. To see Broad Run, turn right onto the side road just before crossing the bridge, then make an immediate left into the small parking area; be careful getting on and off this extremely fast highway. A historical marker stands on the northwest side of the road and across the bridge—on the Union side of the creek, in other words—but the highway traffic makes it inadvisable to stop there.

On October 19, 1863, Stuart and the rest of the Confederate cavalry got one of the last laughs of the war at Buckland Mills.

On the north side of the creek was Union cavalry under two dandies who fancied themselves as skilled as Stuart: General George Custer and General Judson Kilpatrick. Stuart was on the south side providing the rear guard for Lee's army, which was moving south after the nearby Battle of Bristoe Station.

Unknown to Custer and Kilpatrick was the brigade of Confederate general Fitzhugh Lee, which was already several miles nearer Warrenton. Aware that Stuart would be attacked as soon as he pulled back from the creek, Fitz Lee sent him a note saying he

Broad Run, where the Buckland Races started

could set up an ambush. All Stuart had to do was retreat to the ambush site.

Once the ambush was set up at Chesnut Hill, about two miles north of downtown Warrenton on what is now US 15/US 29, Stuart made a big show of being panicked. He ordered his men to forget burning the bridge over Broad Run and to jump on their horses and run back toward Warrenton as if their lives depended on it.

Custer and Kilpatrick bit. As Stuart's supposedly panicked brigade rushed past Chesnut Hill with the Federals in hot pursuit, Fitz Lee's men rose up and fired. Dozens of Federals dropped in the road. Others jumped their horses into a nearby creek, fell off, and drowned under the weight of their equipment. Those Federals who were left turned completely around and fled back the way they had come.

Stuart's Confederates turned around, too. The pursued were now the pursuers. Acting as if they were playing a game, Stuart's men holstered their revolvers and sheathed their sabers. Instead, they concentrated on pulling the panicked Yankees out of their saddles and tossing them on the ground. They kept score on who threw down the most Yankees. More than 250 Federals were captured in the Buckland Races.

Stuart and Fitz Lee couldn't wait to tell General Robert E. Lee about the sport. He needed the laugh, since his infantry had just been mauled at Bristoe Station by a hidden Union division.

Aldie/Middleburg/ Atoka/Upperville

Aldie, Middleburg, Atoka, and Upperville are clustered along US 50 about 50 miles west of Washington, D.C.

In mid-June 1863, Robert E. Lee, buoyed by his victory at Chancellorsville in early May, determined that he would invade the North to attract the attention of both foreign governments and Northerners, who had not suffered as Southerners had. To keep the Federal army occupied while the Army of Northern Virginia prepared to cross the Potomac, he ordered Stuart's cavalry to screen his infantry's movements.

Screening was one of the more important jobs of the cavalry. It served the dual purposes of keeping watch on the opposing army and aggressively harassing that army so its cavalry didn't have time to find out what your own army was doing. Screening meant using your cavalry to help your infantry hide in plain sight.

To screen Lee's advance down the Shenandoah Valley, then north into Pennsylvania, Stuart was ordered to hold several passes in the Bull Run Mountains, which would keep the Federals from crossing into the Shenandoah Valley and discovering Lee heading north.

Aldie Mill, located on U. S. 50

What might be thought of as the first battle of the Pennsylvania Campaign was fought on June 17, 1863, in and around Aldie. Colonel Thomas Munford, commanding Fitz Lee's brigade, was waiting at Aldie when Federal cavalry under General Judson Kilpatrick came thundering down what is now US 50. Fighting past the Aldie Mill—still preserved today—some of the Federals rode up what is now CR 734 (Snickersville Turnpike) in order to capture the gap 1.2 miles away. As the Federals rounded a sharp left-hand turn, they rode right into a single cannon mounted on a hill behind a stone wall that hid dismounted Confederates. Afterward, one Confederate wrote, "I have never seen as many Yankees killed

As the Federals rounded this sharp curve, they rode right into a single cannon mounted on a hill behind a stone wall.

This monument, featuring a horse's head, marks the battle near Aldie.

in the same space of ground in any fight I have ever been."

At this curve on CR 734 today, an attractive monument featuring a horse's head marks the battle spot and lists the names of the dead.

Munford fell back toward Middleburg, located five miles west on US 50. A different troop of Federals slipped past his pickets and headed toward the town, where Stuart and an aide, Major Heros von Borcke, were enjoying the company of ladies. The first they knew of any problem was when one of the few pickets who had not been captured came rushing down the road shouting, "The Yankees are coming!" Stuart aide Henry McClellan delicately wrote that Stuart made "a retreat more rapid than was consistent with dignity and comfort."

Stuart most likely was in or around Chinn's Ordinary—now called The Red Fox Inn—when it came time to flee. The inn is located at 2 East Washington Street in downtown Middleburg. Local historians say that Stuart also discussed the upcoming Pennsylvania Campaign with Colonel John Singleton Mosby, "the Gray

Ghost," at the same inn. The Red Fox certainly has a history of powerful men entertaining ladies. One long-running rumor is that President John F. Kennedy used it as a trysting spot with Marilyn Monroe in the 1960s.

Later on the same day Stuart was driven from town, General Beverly Robertson retook Middleburg from the Federals who had almost captured his boss.

The following day, June 18, Mosby was near Middleburg when he captured a staff officer who was carrying some dispatches that indicated an entire Federal cavalry division of more than 7,000 men was on its way. That force far outnumbered Stuart's men. If they broke through, they could discover Lee on his way north.

That afternoon, Stuart and von Borcke were sitting on their horses on a hill west of Middleburg when that Federal division poured through town. Before withdrawing, the staff officers heard an ominous *whomp*. Looking around to see who'd been hit, they saw von Borcke slump off his horse, blood gushing from a wound in his neck. They got him back on his horse—no easy feat, as von Borcke weighed more than 250 pounds—and sent him to the rear, where he was loaded into an ambulance. As the ambulance bounced westward along what is now US 50, von Borcke rose up from the floor, put his pistol against the driver's head, and ordered him to slow down. At the time of his wounding, von Borcke was wearing a flowing cape and a fancy plumed hat, just like his commander. Stuart complained that the Federals seemed to have been personally targeting him, a breach of military conduct. A historical marker now stands on the hill where von Borcke was wounded.

The small community of Atoka, formerly known as Rector's Crossroads, is located on US 50 at the intersection with CR 773 about four miles west of Middleburg. If you're heading west from Middleburg, turn left on CR 773, stop in front of the country store

In June 1863, Stuart established temporary headquarters in the front yard of this house in Atoka.

at Atoka, and look at the stone house across the road to see an important Stuart site.

It was in June 1863 that Stuart's controversial ties to Lee's Pennsylvania Campaign began to form here at Stuart's temporary headquarters in the front yard of this house. Unwilling to use a private home, and leery of losing a headquarters tent in the event that the Federals staged another lightning raid, Stuart simply threw down a blanket under a tree and declared it his headquarters.

It was in this yard that Stuart awaited the most important orders he would ever receive, orders that would tell him what role he was to play in the upcoming invasion of the North. Already, General Richard Ewell's (formerly Stonewall Jackson's) Second Corps was in Pennsylvania. Longstreet's First Corps and A. P. Hill's Third Corps were on their way north and almost to the Potomac River. Meanwhile, Stuart was guarding the same gaps he had been fighting over for a week. So far, the Federals seemed to have no idea that Lee was invading their territory.

On the morning of June 22, Stuart wrote a note to Lee and Longstreet asking what route he should take into Pennsylvania and what he should do about protecting the mountain gaps. Lee replied at five that afternoon that Stuart should "judge whether you can pass around their army without hindrance, doing them all the damage you can, and cross the river east of the mountains. In either case, after crossing the river, you must move on and feel the right of Ewell's troops, collecting information, provisions, etc. Give instructions to the commander of the brigades left behind, to watch the flank and rear of the army, and (in the event of the enemy leaving their front), retire from the mountains west of the Shenandoah, leaving sufficient pickets to guard the passes and bringing everything clean along the Valley, closing upon the rear of the army. I think the sooner you cross into Maryland, after tomorrow, the better."

The next day, June 23, Mosby returned from a scouting mission and gave Stuart details on the disposition of the Federal army. The Federals were scattered. Stuart could indeed cross the Potomac, get in back of the Union forces, and even come close to threatening Washington. If he moved northward through eastern Pennsylvania, he might be able to accomplish two goals at once: He might further confuse the Federals as to where the main Confederate army was, and he might disrupt the flow of supplies headed to the Federals in Virginia.

On the night of June 23, a courier from Lee rode into the yard with a set of orders marked *Confidential*. Stuart's adjutant, Major Henry McClellan, looked at his sleeping commander and decided he would open the letter to see if Stuart should be awakened. He took one look at the letter from Lee and woke his boss. Stuart told McClellan never to open such mail again, then instructed him to read the letter and/or orders aloud.

This second communication from Lee has always been a point of contention among historians. According to McClellan, writing about the orders nearly 20 years later, it was Lee himself who suggested that Stuart cross the Potomac farther to the east, as the infantry was already crowding the roads around Williamsport, Maryland. The letter also said that Stuart was to meet with General Jubal Early in York, Pennsylvania—the first time Lee had specified a destination.

The reason historians still argue over these orders—and argue about whether Stuart followed them once he started his ride into Pennsylvania—is that they have never turned up in any archives. Apparently, all copies were lost by aides to both Stuart and Lee. Historians generally agree that McClellan was an unlikely person to make up a story about getting such orders from Lee. But the only "proof" of their existence is McClellan's memory two decades later.

On June 24, in response to the previous day's communication, Stuart gave very specific orders of his own to General Beverly Robertson, whose brigade would remain behind with that of General William E. "Grumble" Jones. In those orders, Stuart ordered Robertson (acting as commander of both brigades) to continue to guard the mountain passes. But if the Federals moved, Robertson was to "cross the Potomac and follow the army, keeping on its right and rear." The orders later said to "report anything of importance to Lieutenant General Longstreet," who was, of course, moving into Pennsylvania with Lee.

In effect, Stuart was appointing Robertson, a man he didn't trust, to act in his stead—that is, to act as the trustworthy screen for Lee's army. He left Robertson with about 3,000 men to guard the mountains and then to accompany Lee's army, while Stuart himself took 4,500 troopers on the raid into eastern Pennsylvania.

The number of cavalrymen Lee had access to and his letters to Stuart are important. In Stuart's mind, he was not going off on an adventure behind enemy lines. He was following Lee's orders to attract attention to himself in eastern Pennsylvania while Lee rushed northward through western Pennsylvania. Most important of all, Lee would have nearly half of Stuart's cavalry at his disposal once the infantry crossed the Potomac.

If there was a flaw in Stuart's thinking, it was putting Robertson in command of an important job. In past forays into enemy territory, Stuart had ridden with Robertson's brigade in order to keep an eye on the brigadier's performance. As recently as two weeks earlier, he had blamed Robertson for not giving sufficient warning about the Federal raid across Kelly's Ford, which had resulted in Stuart's near-defeat at Brandy Station. Now, he was giving Robertson virtually an independent command and expecting him to protect the Army of Northern Virginia.

Some critics have suggested that things might have been different had Stuart left Fitz Lee or Wade Hampton behind. Those commanders—particular Fitz Lee, as he was Robert E. Lee's nephew—might have worked more closely with the infantry. But Stuart counted Fitz Lee and Wade Hampton as his best brigadiers, and he wanted his best men along on what he considered the more difficult mission—that of riding behind the Union army. Stuart apparently believed that once he attracted the Federals' attention, they would chase him and forget about looking for Lee's infantry, which would have made Robertson's job easier.

On June 25, Stuart left this yard and headed about 10 miles south to Salem, where he rendezvoused with all of his troopers to begin his most controversial adventure.

The village of Upperville is located on US 50 another 4.5 miles west of the CR 773 junction.

After his wounding on June 18, 1863, Heros von Borcke was taken to a small stone house in Upperville that still stands next to a gas station on the north side of the road. On June 19, Stuart and others came to visit him on what they presumed was his deathbed.

After his wounding on June 1863, Heros Von Borcke was taken to this stone house in Upperville.

But von Borcke fooled everyone and survived, though he was unable to return to field service. He stayed around Richmond until after the war, then moved back to Germany, where he reportedly flew a Confederate flag over his castle until his death. He made one return visit to the United States to see his old friends.

If you care to make a side trip to visit the resting place of a close Stuart associate, continue west about eight miles on US 50, then turn north on US 340 and drive 3.5 miles to Old Chapel, located at the intersection with VA 255. The grave of John Esten Cooke lies in the rear of the cemetery under a large cross.

There was something curious about Stuart's relationship with Cooke, his wife's first cousin. Already well known before the war, Cooke liked serving Stuart as a staff officer. As a writer, he helped contribute to Stuart's reputation by acting as a correspondent to newspapers. It was Cooke who said of Stuart, "No man is more hated and more feared by the Yankees." He also compared Stuart to Garibaldi, the famous Italian who engaged in his own war of independence. Just about everything Cooke wrote concerning Stuart was over the top in admiration and promotion. He helped popularize

The grave of John Esten Cooke is located near Berryville.

the image of Stuart's Ride Around McClellan, writing of "the fun, the frolic, the romance—and the peril too—of that fine journey."

The admiration was not mutual. For some reason, Stuart, the man who virtually invented the word *ego*, felt that Cooke's military skills did not match his own ego. What makes this surprising is that, as a staff officer, Cooke was not expected to have the skills expected of a regimental commander. Stuart made no bones about privately calling Cooke a bore. He even wrote his wife, Flora, and told her as much, though he apparently never confronted Cooke with his true feelings. Meanwhile, Cooke wrote of Stuart as if he were a knight, even composing a song about him. Of all Stuart's staff officers during the war, Cooke served the longest.

Perhaps Cooke eventually learned Stuart's opinion of him. Though he always wrote favorably of Stuart, it was Robert E. Lee and Stonewall Jackson who earned full-scale biographies from Cooke after the war. Stuart, the man Cooke lived with for more than three years, only rated mentions in his books. It would have been natural for Cooke to write the first postwar biography of Stuart, but he left that job to two other staff officers.

John Esten Cooke's home, The Briars

Cooke's home, The Briars, is nearby. If you care to see it, drive one mile south on US 340 and turn right on CR 620. The house is on the left after three miles. It was here that Cooke wrote many of his books.

Chancellorsville

The site of Lee's greatest victory, which would not have come about if not for Stuart, is about 12 miles west of Fredericksburg on VA 3. Admission to this National Park Service site also covers visits to the battlefields at Fredericksburg and Spotsylvania. Battlefield maps are available at the visitor center. Call 540-373-6122 for information.

The Battle of Chancellorsville must have stood out in Stuart's memory for the rest of his life. On the first day, he lost one of his best staff officers. On the second day, he delivered news to Lee and Jackson that would be used to launch Jackson's Flank March. On the third day, Stuart, temporarily acting as a corps commander, finished what Jackson had started on the second day. Though Stuart was directly responsible for one of the major Confederate victories of the war, it did not translate into a promotion to lieutenant general, an honor he thought he deserved.

By May 1, 1863, the Union army, camped on the banks of the Rappahannock River north of Fredericksburg since December, had almost completed a lightning movement west of the city. The Federals, commanded by General Joseph Hooker, had crossed the river and were preparing to bear down on Lee's left flank.

Stonewall Jackson's corps rushed to the rescue, hitting Hooker's advance line so hard at a house called Chancellorsville that Hooker assumed he was feeling the full weight of the Southern army. In fact, Jackson had only about a fifth of the men the Federals did. Hooker pulled his men back and started digging trenches.

Stuart and Jackson spent much of May 1 together. Near the end of the day, they were around Catherine Furnace, a small, abandoned iron refinery at the west end of Furnace Road, when Jackson decided he wanted to reach some high ground in order to see what

Catherine Furnace

Hazel Grove, where Federal fire almost wounded Stuart and Jackson

PHOTO COURTESY OF NATIONAL PARK SERVICE

the Federals were doing. What puzzled the Confederate generals was that the Federals seemed to be digging in, rather than advancing. The heavy woods kept Jackson from seeing what was happening and from allowing Confederate infantry to advance very far.

From Catherine Furnace, they rode north toward Hazel Grove for approximately a half-mile along a tiny path hardly wide enough to qualify as a road. That path, swallowed over the years, was located near the National Park Service road that leads from Catherine Furnace to Hazel Grove.

Jackson asked Stuart's horse artillery to fire a few rounds into the woods to try to clear a path for some supporting infantry Jackson had nearby. Almost instantly, masked Federal batteries on Hazel Grove Ridge returned the fire. Stuart shouted to Jackson, "We must move from here!" as shells fired blindly by the Federals exploded only yards from the two generals.

Both men continued to lead charmed lives—for the moment, at least. Earlier in the war, Jackson had received a broken finger from a Federal bullet, and Stuart had half his mustache removed by Union fire. But neither had been seriously wounded.

Not everyone was so lucky in the exchange at Chancellorsville. As the two generals retreated, a shell fragment hit behind the knee of Major Channing Price, Stuart's adjutant, or secretary. Price declared that his wound was not serious, but it must have severed an artery, for he soon fell from the saddle and quickly bled to death. Jackson's own adjutant noted that Jackson was "detained for a short time" over the "sad incident," as if he felt responsible for alerting the Federal artillery that it had a target. Stuart, too, was brokenhearted. Just a month earlier, he had lost John Pelham, the commander of his horse artillery. The deaths of Pelham and Price were similar. Both were in their early 20s; tiny pieces of shrapnel mortally wounded both in places that were not even visible at first glance; and Stuart considered them both very important. Pelham had no peer when it came to operating cannons. Price had no peer when turning Stuart's oral dictation into orders. He had learned to write precisely by taking dictation for his businessman father, who was blind.

After the death of Price, Stuart ordered everyone on his staff to carry tourniquets in their pockets. He believed, probably correctly, that Price could have been saved had someone shut off the flow of blood from the severed artery. Price's wounding was similar to one suffered by General Albert Sidney Johnson at Shiloh, Tennessee, in April 1862. Both men ignored wounds that severed arteries, and both bled to death when no tourniquet was applied to their legs.

Sadly, Stuart's relationship with Channing Price's brother, Tom, quickly collapsed. Tom, a perennial student who would rather have sat out the war at a university in Paris or Berlin, kept a diary while serving on Stuart's staff. In it, he complained of Stuart's gregariousness, making him seem a happy bore. The diary was captured and parts of it published in the *New York Times*. Stuart had Price transferred to the engineers.

A second Stuart site at Chancellorsville is located at the corner of Furnace Road and Old Plank Road (CR 610). It was here on the evening of May 1 that Lee and Jackson had a private conversation trying to figure out what they could do to dislodge Hooker's Federals from their trenches. They dispatched their engineering officers to scout as close as possible to the Union lines to determine if there were weaknesses. Both generals knew that the lines were strong, but they hoped the engineers would find some sort of break that they could exploit.

Before the engineers could return, Stuart arrived with news that he credited to General Fitzhugh Lee, one of his brigade commanders and Robert E. Lee's nephew. While riding along the Federal right flank, Fitz Lee had discovered it was "in the

The site of Lee and Jackson's last meeting, where Stuart delivered his scouting report

The site where Jackson's flank attack opened up at Chancellorsville

air," meaning that it was not anchored to anything—such as the Rappahannock River or a ravine—that would provide natural cover. Normally, generals had their men dig trenches to provide artificial anchors, but Union general Oliver O. Howard, commander of the 11th Corps, had not bothered with basic military procedure.

Stuart had just solved the problem Lee and Jackson thought had no answer. As if to reinforce the value of Stuart's information, the two engineers returned with word that the Union left was firmly anchored on the river and that the center regiments were dug in behind deep trenches.

Lee ordered his cavalry chief to start scouting known roads and to locate other roads that did not show up on the map in order to find a way to transport a large portion of the Confederate army to the Federal right wing.

While Stuart was gone, the owners of Catherine Furnace told Jackson about a newly built road that was out of sight of Federal pickets. They subsequently led Jackson to the Federal right wing, Stuart's troops following to screen the movement of the infantry. Curious Union pickets watched the Confederate horsemen seeming to head in the direction of Richmond. They didn't realize that another road out of their sight led to their army's far right flank.

Stuart's troopers did not participate in the flank attack. Soon after it began, they moved directly north to Ely's Ford on the Rapidan in anticipation of fighting back a rumored cavalry assault.

To reach the third significant Stuart site at Chancellorsville, drive east on Bullock Road from the visitor center, turn left on Ely's Ford Road (CR 610), and drive about 3.5 miles to the historical marker just before the road heads down to cross the Rapidan River.

It was on this hill that Stuart discovered a Union infantry regiment guarding the ford below. He fired a few volleys and was preparing an attack when a member of A. P. Hill's force arrived with startling news around 10 P.M. on May 2: Jackson had been wounded less than an hour earlier. Hill, Jackson's senior division commander, had also been wounded near the same spot, by an artillery shell fragment.

Sometime around midnight, Stuart left his cavalry and rode off to assume command of Jackson's Second Corps. There is something curious about this. No one in a senior capacity apparently told him to do it. Hill, the acting commander of the corps after Jackson's

Ely's Ford, where Stuart took command of Jackson's Second Corps

wounding, did not have that kind of power. Robert E. Lee, seemingly the only man who could have offered command of the Second Corps to Stuart, did not issue such an order. One account says that Major Sandie Pendleton, Jackson's adjutant, was the officer who sent for Stuart, the closest major general. True, Stuart had the rank, but he was in an entirely different branch of the army, was not aware where Jackson's troops were on the field, and had no idea what Jackson had been planning. By rights, Jackson's other division officers—particularly General Robert Rodes, the senior general of the corps who had opened the flank attack—should have been in line to take over the Second Corps. But he acquiesced when Stuart showed up, probably thinking that Stuart had been ordered by Lee to take over the corps. In reality, Lee gave no such order. By most accounts, he did not learn of Jackson's wounding until 2:30 A.M. on May 3, at least two hours after Stuart had taken command of the Second Corps and nearly six hours after Jackson's wounding. Around three that morning, Lee wrote Stuart, ordering that "the glorious victory thus far achieved be prosecuted with the utmost vigor and the enemy given no time to rally." He addressed Stuart as the commander of the corps, though he had not officially been given that distinction.

Stuart did press the attack, taking the high ground of Fairview and Hazel Grove—the same area where Union batteries had almost killed him and Jackson two days earlier. From that high ground, Confederate colonel Edward Porter Alexander, now reporting to Stuart, massed cannons that were able to reach Hooker's headquar- ters. Once the Confederate cannons started firing on Federal headquarters, the Union resistance collapsed. The attack by Stuart could not have gone better if Jackson himself had been in command. As the Federals swarmed back across the Rappahannock, Lee realized he had won the most complete victory of the war to that date.

W. W. Blackford, Stuart's adjutant, wrote that, at Chancellorsville, Stuart "displayed a military genius and heroism surpassed by few characters in history." Stuart certainly thought so. He reportedly took time before the battle to change into a different uniform and sash so as to distinguish himself from being a cavalry officer. He acted a little rashly during the battle. Once, he charged directly at a Federal line and ordered it to stop firing into his men. In the confusion over who he was, the Federal line obeyed the orders of a Confederate major general.

After the battle, Stuart quietly lobbied Lee for a promotion to lieutenant general. While Lee praised him, he did not offer permanent command of any corps. Instead of promoting Stuart, Lee offered to make the cavalry command larger, which seemed to mollify Stuart once he realized Lee had no intention of allowing him to leave the cavalry for the infantry.

Verdiersville

The small, unmarked community of Verdiersville is located about 10 miles east of Orange on VA 20. Just east of the cluster of businesses, turn north on CR 621 (Pine Stake Road) and drive 0.9 mile, watching on the right for a two-story brick house virtually masked by trees. This is a private home; do not trespass. It was here that the South almost lost Stuart a full two years before he was killed in battle.

After the Battle of Cedar Mountain on August 9, 1862, Robert E. Lee pulled his army back to Orange and Gordonsville to figure out what to do next. He needed to strike at Union general

John Pope's Army of Virginia, then near Culpeper, before Union general George McClellan could pull away from the Virginia Peninsula and merge with Pope. If that merger occurred, Lee would be outnumbered nearly three to one. He could not hope to stop such a massive opponent.

On top of that, Lee had a particular hate for Pope, whom he called a "miscreant," probably the only time he ever referred to anyone on the other side in a derogatory manner. Pope had instituted a policy of harassing, evicting, and arresting civilians, sometimes forcing women and children off their land even though there was no military reason for such action. Lee had always been careful to wage civilized war against his military foes, but civilians in his beloved Virginia were not being granted the same courtesy.

Lee soon found an opportunity to strike Pope. Apparently, an unnamed Confederate officer operating from an observation post on Clark's Mountain east of Orange (a location that is now private property) saw what he knew to be an opportunity and reported it to Lee. After Cedar Mountain, Pope had slowly but surely started moving his army south. In doing so, he crept deeper into a V-shaped section of land created by the convergence of the Rappahannock River northeast of Culpeper and the Rapidan River southwest of Orange. The two rivers met about 12 miles west of Fredericksburg.

Called to Clark's Mountain by the observer, Lee and Longstreet saw that Pope was marching into a trap of his own making. If Lee could send Stuart's cavalry to the rear of Pope to burn a railroad bridge over the Rappahannock, and if Stuart's men then swept onto the Union army's rear, Lee himself could attack from the southwest flank. With rivers on two sides of him, Confederate cavalry in his rear, and Confederate infantry in his front and on his flanks, Pope would be in a box.

The key to the strategy was having the cavalry burn the bridge and fall in behind Pope. Unfortunately, this created a problem. The cavalry was scattered around Richmond, its closest elements at least 30 miles away. When Lee gave Stuart his orders at Orange Court House on August 17, Stuart literally had no troops with him, only aides. Anticipating that Lee would need cavalry, he had already ordered General Fitzhugh Lee's brigade to Raccoon Ford on the Rapidan.

Stuart subsequently rode here to Verdiersville, which was on Fitz Lee's route to Raccoon Ford. Stuart planned to show him the secret orders he had just received from Robert E. Lee, Fitz's uncle.

When Stuart arrived in the village and stopped at the two-story brick home belonging to the Rhodes family, he was puzzled to learn that the aides he had sent ahead to intercept Fitz Lee had not encountered him. Stuart must have been squirming. Robert E. Lee was counting on him to launch the battle, yet the troops needed to do that were nowhere in sight.

Stuart figured he could do little more than wait for Fitz Lee. He lay down on the porch, using his crimson-lined cloak as a pillow and carefully placing his hat—newly won in a bet with a Yankee friend—beside him. Before he went to sleep, he sent an aide,

The house where Stuart lost his cape, hat, and more importantly, Lee's orders

Norman Fitzhugh, down the road to wait for Fitz Lee. That was a mistake. In Fitzhugh's satchel were the secret orders detailing the placement of the Confederate cavalry.

Before dawn, two regiments of Union cavalry caught Fitzhugh and his satchel near Verdiersville. Stuart, hearing horsemen approaching but assuming them to be Confederates, sent another couple of aides, including John Singleton Mosby, down the road to meet the riders. Mosby soon came rushing back firing his pistol into the dawn mist. Without grabbing his cape or hat, Stuart leaped aboard his horse, Skylark, and rode out of danger. The last he saw his hat, it was being tossed around on the sabers of the Federals.

But far more important than the loss of the hat was the loss of the orders. When the Federals read the contents of Fitzhugh's satchel, they forwarded them immediately to Pope. Considered a fool by many Union as well as Confederate commanders, Pope finally recognized the trap in which he had placed himself.

When Robert E. Lee learned that his orders had been captured, he went to the Clark's Mountain observation post and saw Pope pulling his army back north of the Rappahannock. Lee's great trap, which would almost certainly have been the most effective maneuver of the war, would never be sprung.

Stuart spent several days wearing nothing but a handkerchief on his head. Even his men could not resist shouting at him, "Where's your hat?" even though they knew the story of how he had almost been captured.

Stuart was already planning his revenge. He would get it in a few days at a place called Catlett's Station.

Stuart was almost caught in a vise at Jack's Shop, which is present-day Rochelle.

Rochelle

Rochelle, formerly called Jack's Shop, is located about 20 miles northeast of Charlottesville on VA 231. Look for the historical markers on the north side of the community.

As the war wore on, the Confederate cavalry found itself almost constantly tested. When Confederate general James Longstreet's First Corps of infantry left in early September 1863 to head west for detached service under General Braxton Bragg at Chickamauga, Union general George Meade's intelligence soon discovered the move. He decided to press Lee's army, which was still recovering from Gettysburg, a battle fought two months earlier.

One test came when Stuart learned through his intelligence that Union general John Buford, who had slowed Lee just enough on the first day at Gettysburg, was riding toward him with a full division of cavalry. Stuart moved out to meet him. They ran into each other at Jack's Shop.

What Stuart did not know was that Buford's men comprised only half the Union force, since General Judson Kilpatrick's division was riding toward Jack's Shop from the south. Stuart was about to be caught in a vise.

He did the only thing he could: He attacked in both directions. Unlimbering his horse artillery on a small hill located across from where the historical markers stand today, Stuart pointed them at both opposing forces. The Federals were surprised. Kilpatrick's men melted in the face of the attack on their front, which opened a hole back toward Stuart's headquarters at Liberty Mills, located where VA 231 and US 20 intersect today.

After being surprised at Brandy Station, then drawing criticism for being out of touch at Gettysburg, and now being surrounded at Jack's Shop, Stuart found that his reputation among his fellow commanders and the general public was at its lowest. He didn't even bother writing a report on the affair at Jack's Shop. It would have been too embarrassing.

Cedar Mountain

Located about five miles south of Culpeper on US 15, the Cedar Mountain battlefield looks much like it did on August 9, 1862, when Stonewall Jackson clashed with Union general Nathaniel Banks. Look for the intersection of US 15 and CR 691 (Carver School Road). The red-brick farmhouse flanked by silos on the east side of this intersection was Jackson's headquarters during the action. It was here that he met Stuart after the battle.

Cedar Mountain, where tradition says Stuart got his plumed hat

Though the Confederates achieved a victory at Cedar Mountain, it cannot be said that they accomplished their purpose, since the Union army was still firmly in place. Following the battle, Robert E. Lee had to lay plans for Second Manassas to get at the Federals.

Stonewall Jackson would have appreciated Stuart's services at Cedar Mountain, but instead he had those of General Beverly Robertson, who Stuart complained was one of the most "troublesome" men he ever had in the cavalry. Robertson's inactivity during the battle is proved by the fact that only one cavalryman was killed in action that claimed hundreds of infantrymen on both sides.

When Stuart arrived at Jackson's headquarters after the battle, Jackson asked him to scout where the rest of the Union army was, in case Banks or the rest of John Pope's army might be planning to attack again the following day. Stuart rode off toward Culpeper and found that the bulk of the Federals were little more than six miles away. That information would come in handy over the next couple of weeks.

Two days after the battle, Jackson and Banks still faced each other. They called a truce to bury the dead, who were rotting in the extreme heat. During the truce, three Union generals who had known Stuart when he was a young lieutenant fighting Indians in Kansas and Texas came over to renew acquaintances with their now-famous friend. They brought a box lunch and a bottle of wine and essentially ignored the grim task of the burial crews operating all around them.

Eventually, the course of the conversation turned to the just-completed battle and how the newspapers invariably got things wrong. Stuart bet Union general Samuel Crawford a new hat that the Northern newspapers would proclaim Cedar Mountain a Union victory. Crawford exclaimed that not even the notably inaccurate *New York Herald* could produce a victory out of the clear defeat Banks had just suffered.

Several days later, a package was passed through the Confederate lines. In it were a copy of the *Herald* discussing the great Union victory at Cedar Mountain and a new plumed hat. Stuart tradition says this was the start of the general's wearing of plumed hats, though he kept that particular hat for little more than a week.

Brandy Station/Beverly Ford/Kelly's Ford

> *The site of the largest cavalry battle ever waged on the North American continent is just off US 29 about eight miles north of Culpeper. Beverly Ford and Kelly's Ford are located nearby on the Rappahannock River.*

Though Stuart never admitted it, the Battle of Brandy Station on June 9, 1863, came close to being his undoing as a Southern hero. The South barely squeaked by with a victory because Stuart had worn his men down with a showy review mostly for the ladies and because he allowed his command to be surprised. He also put his commanding general in the line of fire. Had it not been for the advance of infantry from Culpeper, Stuart might have lost Brandy Station, and Lee himself might have been captured.

On June 5, 1863, Stuart staged a massive cavalry review on a ridge behind where the Virginia State Highway Patrol station stands today, two miles south of Brandy Station on CR 762, which runs east of and closely parallel to US 29. His stated objective was to demonstrate the strength of his 10,000-man force to Robert E. Lee, who had not needed the cavalry for his May victory at Chancellorsville. When Lee could not come that particular day because he was still moving the infantry, Stuart held the review anyway for a wide variety of women and dignitaries, some of whom rode by special train to see the extravaganza. It must have taken more than an hour for the massed formations to ride by. Following that came mock charges on the horse artillery. Even the common soldiers who grumbled about it being a waste of ammunition and horseflesh had to agree that, as spectacle, the review was impressive.

Two days later, Lee told Stuart he would be glad to review the cavalry. The next day—just three days after the first review—Stuart assembled the men for Lee. This time, the review was staged a mile up the road, closer to Brandy Station, at a spot noted by a historical marker on CR 762. The women were absent, and the grumbling was louder. When Stuart appeared with his horse bedecked in flowers, Lee deflated him with a comment on how John Pope once reviewed his troops on a flower-decorated horse. He said he hoped Stuart wouldn't share Pope's fate.

To see the site of Stuart's headquarters at Fleetwood Hill,

The site where Stuart assembled a massive cavalry review for Lee

continue on CR 762 to Brandy Station, turn west on CR 663, cross US 29, and turn right on CR 685. After a mile on CR 685, pull over where some steps on the right side of the road lead to a historical marker. This is the headquarters site. Holding Fleetwood Hill was the turning point of the battle. It was here that Stuart aide Henry McClellan held off Union general David Gregg's first attack with a single small howitzer. Fooled into thinking the hill was heavily defended, Gregg delayed his attack. Finally, a regiment of Confederates arrived to go saber to saber with the Federals fighting for the crest of the hill.

Note the large house on the hill in the distance. That is Barbour House, where Lee watched the progress of the Battle of Brandy Station. If the Federals had taken this hill, Lee would have been unprotected.

Continue another 0.8 mile on CR 685, then turn left onto CR 676, which passes the airport. The road's designation changes to CR 677; the dirt CR 677 finally dead-ends at private property. This spot is close to Beverly Ford, where the battle began before dawn when cavalry under Union general John Buford splashed across the Rappahannock River, surprising the brigade of Confederate

The site of Stuart's headquarters at
Fleetwood Hill

Kelly's Ford, where Union troops crossed
behind schedule

general William E. "Grumble" Jones. Jones's men had to fight half-
dressed from horses that were not even saddled.

Thankfully for Stuart, the second prong of the Union attack,
under the command of General David Gregg, was late in crossing
Kelly's Ford, located about 10 miles east. General Beverly
Robertson, one of Stuart's brigadiers, was also unable to stop the
Federals. In fact, he and his men remained hidden in the woods as
they watched most of the Federals pass.

Both prongs of the Federal assault were aimed at Fleetwood Hill.

The road Union troops followed from Beverly Ford to the Brandy Station battlefield

As you return from the Beverly Ford area on the dirt road, you'll be following the route of the Federal attack. Watch for a broad, sweeping curve shortly before the paved road begins. It was here that Colonel Benjamin "Grimes" Davis, a Southerner who had stayed with the Union, was shot out of the saddle. Just nine months earlier, Davis had led the Federal cavalry out of Stonewall Jackson's trap at Harpers Ferry.

At the intersection with the paved CR 676, turn right and drive to the site of the old St. James Church, where the Confederates put up a spirited defense to hold off Buford. At the end of the day, Buford and Gregg recrossed the river, bruised but satisfied that they had hurt—and embarrassed—the Confederates.

Stuart never admitted to being surprised at Brandy Station. In fact, he claimed it as a great victory. But observers of the battle said otherwise. Even some of the ladies he had entertained earlier in the week accused Stuart of being recklessly inattentive to the threat that had been right across the river the whole time.

This was one of the last great cavalry battles of history. It saw a total of 10,000 men frequently swinging sabers at each other, as had been done hundreds of years earlier. Whenever they had a chance to reload, they fired pistols or carbines. But for much of the day, there was no time.

One thing that was obvious after the battle was that the Federal cavalry, once the laughingstock of the Union army, was now able to match the skill of the Confederates. That was due in large measure to the efforts of David Gregg, perhaps the one man who equaled Stuart at commanding cavalry.

Gregg had been left an orphan at age 14 when his parents were struck down by fever. Raised by an uncle, he won an appointment to West Point in 1851. Two years ahead of him was Phil Sheridan, his future cavalry compatriot. One year ahead was Stuart, his future adversary. After graduating near the top of his class in 1855, Gregg probably could have become an engineer, as most top students did. Instead, he chose the Dragoons, a type of mounted infantry that would soon be converted into cavalry. Gregg spent most of his prewar service in Washington State, where he engaged in several fierce Indian fights. He was never stationed with Stuart.

When the war started, Gregg returned east to head a regiment of Pennsylvanians. During early operations against Confederates like Stuart, he began to complain to superiors of "cavalry misuse." He thought that the Federals used their cavalrymen poorly

The Brandy Station Battlefield

by making them mounted escorts for the infantry. After watching men like Stuart raid wagon trains and destroy telegraph lines behind Federal lines, he came to believe that it would take the adoption of just such tactics by the Federals before they would start to match the skills of the Confederates.

Early in 1863, the Federals began to make the first tentative moves toward creating the independent force Gregg advocated. It was at Brandy Station that his dream of a fully capable Federal cavalry became a reality. Since the Federals left the field, Brandy Station was technically a Union defeat, but for the first time, the Union cavalry had done serious damage to the Confederate cavalry, both in casualties and reputation.

If you'd like to make a short side trip to the site where one of Stuart's favorite soldiers was mortally wounded, drive 2.1 miles north from Brandy Station on US 15/US 29 and turn right on CR 674 in Elkwood. Follow CR 674 for 3.8 miles to a gravel parking lot on the left; this lot lies 0.8 mile before Kelly's Ford, used frequently by both the Confederates and the Federals to cross the Rappahannock. Walk past the gate and follow the trail for about a half-mile. The stone wall visible on the right was part of a Confederate defensive line. Walk until you see a marker for Major John Pelham on the left of the trail. If you're visiting in the summertime, make sure you check for ticks after making this trek.

Pelham never got the chance to graduate from West Point. The war erupted just weeks before he would have received his diploma. He found his place with Stuart as the head of the cavalry's "horse artillery." He even captured the attention of Robert E. Lee at Fredericksburg. Watching Pelham and just his two cannons hold up the entire Federal attack on Jackson's flank, Lee remarked, "It is good to see courage in one so young." Stuart loved Pelham like a

The marker placed where Major John Pelham was mortally wounded.

little brother. He saw in him a younger version of himself, somewhat rebellious, somewhat innovative.

Pelham was at Kelly's Ford as an observer on March 17, 1863, when a Federal patrol attacked. A companion was speaking to Pelham when the young major keeled over flat on his back. There did not seem to be a mark on him. The companion found a tiny hole in the back of his head, the result of a piece of shrapnel from an exploding shell hitting him. Pelham died the next day in a house in Culpeper.

Reports circulated after his death that three different young women around the South claimed they were engaged to Pelham. All three went into mourning.

Staunton

The school now known as Stuart Hall was founded as the Virginia Female Institute in 1844. It is located at 235 West Frederick Street in Staunton, which is just off I-81 in the central Shenandoah Valley.

Stuart Hall, formerly Virginia Female Institute, where Mrs. General J. E. B. Stuart taught for 19 years
PHOTO COURTESY OF STUART HALL

Flora Cooke Stuart never remarried after the death of her husband in 1864. She marked his memory in the custom of the time, by wearing black for the rest of her life. Refusing her father's offer to move north, she stayed true to her promise to her husband that she would always live in the South and raise and educate their children there. She preferred to be called Mrs. General J. E. B. Stuart.

For a while, Flora lived in the town of Saltville in southwestern Virginia, where her brother-in-law helped her open a small cabin school so she could support herself and her family by teaching. In 1880, she accepted an offer from the Virginia Female Institute to move to Staunton and become the school's principal. She remained for 19 years before retiring to her daughter's home in Norfolk. In 1907, the school was renamed Stuart Hall in her honor. She died on May 10, 1923. That was 60 years to the day after the death of her husband's friend and boss, Stonewall Jackson, and 59 years minus two days after the death of Stuart himself.

The Dabbs House

RICHMOND AREA

Richmond/Blackstone

Richmond is located at the junction of I-64 and I-95. The Dabbs House is at the eastern edge of the downtown area, on Nine Mile Road just north of Exit 193 off I-64. Several other Stuart sites are downtown. Blackstone lies about 40 miles southwest of the city.

The Dabbs House, Robert E. Lee's June 1862 headquarters where he planned the Seven Days' Campaign, is located at 3820 Nine Mile Road. Restored to its wartime appearance, it is now a police headquarters; no public tours are offered. Several historical markers stand in front of the house.

Stuart had probably not seen Lee in person for any length of time for two and a half years before meeting him at the Dabbs House on June 10, 1862. The last occasion they had served together was the capture of John Brown at Harpers Ferry in October 1859.

Now, Stuart, a cadet at West Point when Lee was superintendent, was here discussing with his old mentor how to scout the disposition of Union general George McClellan's Army of the Potomac on the Virginia Peninsula. Stuart reported that one of his men, John Singleton Mosby, who would later gain fame as "the Gray Ghost" while leading his own band of partisan rangers, had done enough scouting behind Union lines to suspect that McClellan was not properly protecting his supply line. An interested Lee ordered Stuart and his cavalry to find exactly where McClellan's men were north of the Chickahominy River.

On June 12, Stuart left with 1,200 men on what would become known as the "Ride Around McClellan." When he returned to this same house on June 15, he had 1,199 men, having lost only one cavalryman on an 80-mile ride completely around McClellan's army. Stuart confirmed for Lee what he had suspected: that McClellan's right flank north of the Chickahominy was vulnerable to attack, as it was separated from the bulk of the Union army by the river. Based on this information, Lee moved the bulk of his army to Mechanicsville and launched the Seven Days' Campaign 10 days later.

Stuart's hat, gloves, and LeMat revolver are on display at the Museum of the Confederacy, located at the corner of 12th and Clay Streets in downtown Richmond. To get there from the Dabbs House, drive west on I-64, then head south on I-95 and look for signs for the museum.

For unknown reasons, Stuart was not carrying his LeMat on the day of his mortal wounding. The hat is presumably a replacement for the one he lost to a Federal patrol at Verdiersville. The lost hat had been a gift from an old friend in the Union ranks. Stuart replaced it with any number of plumed hats to enhance his image.

One interesting Stuart-related artifact at the museum belonged to Heros von Borcke, a Stuart aide. Von Borcke was a Prussian who ran the blockade just to fight for the Confederacy. A huge man at over six feet and 250 pounds, he owned a custom-made cavalry sword that is on display next to a puny sword sported by a much smaller French general who also fought for the South. Von Borcke wrote in his postwar book that he used this sword to decapitate a Federal at Brandy Station.

While you're in downtown Richmond, you'll also want to see the Stuart artifacts held at the Virginia Historical Society, located at 438 North Boulevard. From the Museum of the Confederacy, go one block south to Broad Street and turn right, or west. Follow Broad to Robinson Avenue, turn left, drive to Kensington Avenue, and turn right. The historical society is on the left at the corner of Kensington and Boulevard.

It is here that you'll find the last artifacts associated with J. E. B. Stuart, including his uniform, his sash, and the .36 caliber Whitney pistol he was carrying the day he was shot. Some of Stuart's blood is on the sash. The .36 Whitney is a curious Stuart artifact, as he was known to carry a much larger .44 LeMat pistol. Also on display is a bowie knife Stuart took as a souvenir from John Brown in 1859. Brown himself took it from a militia-man at the Battle of Black Jack in Kansas in 1856. That militiaman was later killed at Yellow Tavern, the same battle in which Stuart was mortally wounded. Brown used the knife as a pattern for the pikes he made with the intention of arming the slaves.

From the historical society, drive one block east to Monument Avenue, turn right, and go to the corner of Lombardy Street to see a large, impressive statue of Stuart erected in 1907. Perhaps it is fitting that Stuart's statue shows considerable dash compared to the more sedate likenesses of Lee, Jackson, Davis, and Maury, the

Statue of Stuart on Monument Avenue

other Confederates on the avenue.

From Monument Avenue, turn right onto Belvidere Street and follow the signs to Hollywood Cemetery, the last resting place of a number of Confederate heroes. During office hours, you can obtain a map pointing out important graves. Even if you don't have a map, the blue line painted on the road will lead you to the historical sections of the cemetery. The graves of Stuart and his family are in a curve on Ellis Avenue along the blue line.

On May 11, 1864, Stuart was shot in the stomach at Yellow Tavern, approximately 10 miles north of the city. He was taken to downtown Richmond and the home of Dr. Charles Brewer at 206 West Grace Street, where he died on May 12. Unfortunately, the house was torn down in 1893; the area is now a commercial district. Ironically, Stuart had stopped at Dr. Brewer's when he joined the Confederate army in May 1861. It was thus at the same home that he came into the Confederacy and left it four years later.

Dr. Brewer, married to Stuart's wife's sister, knew, as did the other doctors present, that there was absolutely nothing they could do for Stuart. A .44 caliber pistol bullet had perforated his intes-

Graves of J. E. B. and Flora Stuart in Hollywood Cemetery

tines and damaged arteries. The doctors knew that even if they could figure a way to close off the arteries, peritonitis would kill Stuart within hours.

One of Stuart's visitors was von Borcke, who had been shot in the neck in June 1863. Every doctor who had looked at von Borcke's wound had told him that he would die, yet he had survived. The still-jovial Stuart played off that experience when von Borcke entered the room. "I don't think I'm as badly wounded as you were, and I hope I'll get over it as you did," he said.

Von Borcke dashed off a telegram to Flora Stuart, who was staying on a plantation about 30 miles northeast of the city. It took hours for it to reach her, as the Federals had torn down telegraph lines during the raid on Yellow Tavern. Once Flora got the telegram, she began trying to reach the city on a locomotive, only to discover that the Federals had also torn up track north of Richmond. At Ashland, someone borrowed a carriage so she could continue the journey. Once, a sentry stopped the carriage and demanded to know why it was in such a rush. When told, the sentry replied that he had tried to fire two chambers of his pistol at the carriage when no one answered his challenge, which could not be heard over the ongoing thunderstorm.

While Flora was still frantically on her way, Stuart was fading fast. President Jefferson Davis paid a visit. Stuart told him, "I am willing to die, if God and my country think I have fulfilled my destiny and my duty." He gave away his two remaining horses to two staff members and even decided who should get which horse by asking which was the heavier officer. When an Episcopal pastor entered the room, Stuart asked everyone to join him in singing "Rock of Ages."

As the day wore into afternoon, Stuart asked Dr. Brewer if he would survive into the evening. Brewer told him no. He asked for Flora several times, but no one could honestly tell him where she was on the journey to his side.

At 7:38 P.M. on May 12, 1864, Stuart turned to Brewer and said, "I am going fast now. God's will be done." They were his last words. It was past 10:30 when Flora finally arrived. By the quiet surrounding the house, she knew she was too late to be with her husband on his deathbed.

In going through Stuart's pockets, his aides found a lock of his dead daughter's hair, a poem—clipped from a newspaper—about children dying before their time, and several orders. Among them was the order he had written to Jackson's corps congratulating it upon winning the Battle of Chancellorsville a year earlier. Stuart had harbored the hope he would be named a lieutenant general and get command of that corps, but Lee kept him a major general in command of the cavalry.

Later that night, Robert E. Lee, then fighting at Spotsylvania

Court House, was told of Stuart's death. He said to his staff, "I can hardly think of him without weeping." He also said something that seemed to vindicate Stuart for any perceived lapse in judgment during the Pennsylvania Campaign: "He never brought me a false piece of information."

The funeral was held the next day at St. James Episcopal Church; the original church building no longer stands. Stuart was then taken to Hollywood Cemetery. One year earlier, Stonewall Jackson had lain in state in the governor's mansion. But there was no such honor for Stuart. The city was under attack. During the funeral service, cannons boomed all around Richmond.

Continue following the blue line through the cemetery until you reach Davis Circle, were President Jefferson Davis is buried. Right across the circle from him is the grave of General Fitzhugh Lee, one of Stuart's best friends from West Point and one of his finest brigadiers.

You might also want to find the burial spot of Major Richard Channing Price, a Stuart aide who was killed at Chancellorsville in May 1863. He is buried in Section E, Lot 106. Stuart considered Price one of his best aides. He had the uncanny ability to listen to Stuart without taking any notes, then, when composing orders, write down exactly what Stuart had said.

It is worth noting that the grave of perhaps the most controversial of Stuart's subordinates is located outside the Richmond area. The remains of General Beverly Holcombe Robertson lie near the intersection of US 460 and VA 153 about six miles northeast of the village of Blackstone, 40 miles southwest of the capital. As the grave is difficult to find and on private property, it is not recommended that you go looking for it.

Robertson may have been the most disliked man in the Confederate cavalry. About the only people who liked him were his

Gravesite of Beverly Holcombe Robertson

friends in the old army—the United States Army, that is.

Though he was Stuart's senior by less than six years, Robertson looked much older, thanks to his balding head and cold eyes. A lackluster graduate of the class of 1849 at West Point, Robertson fought Indians on the frontier, where he undoubtedly ran into Stuart. At one time, his commander was Colonel Phillip St. George Cooke, Stuart's future father-in-law. Robertson, a Virginian, liked the United States Army so much that he considered staying in, perhaps at the urging of his old commander Cooke, also a Virginian. Robertson did not resign his army commission until August 8, 1861, nearly four months after the war began and a full two weeks after First Manassas. This reluctance to join the Confederacy haunted his entire career, as his fellow Southern officers never quite trusted his commitment to the cause.

Though Robertson was elected colonel of the Fourth Virginia Cavalry, his belief in strict discipline did not make him popular in the rest of the cavalry. Dislike for him grew when President Jefferson Davis appointed Robertson to take over the command of Stonewall Jackson's cavalry upon the death of Turner Ashby. Jackson tolerated Robertson for a while but eventually found a way to transfer him to North Carolina. Kicked back to Virginia after his commander in North Carolina found his brigade to be "wonderfully inefficient," Robertson found himself directly under Stuart.

Robertson could never do much right for Stuart. His troops were brushed aside at Kelly's Ford in the opening fighting at Brandy Station in June 1863, a failure that almost cost Stuart the battle. Robertson's men did very little fighting that day, losing only four horses and no men to combat. Had it not been for the stubborn defense mounted by Stuart's aides and couriers with the help of a single cannon, Union cavalry would have taken Stuart's headquarters.

Two weeks later, as the cavalry was preparing to enter Pennsylvania, Robertson's brigade was routed at Upperville. That was one more strike against Robertson in Stuart's eyes. Rather than bring such an inefficient brigade along on the Pennsylvania ride, he ordered Robertson to take overall command of his brigade and that belonging to William E. "Grumble" Jones. Both were then detached from Stuart's cavalry to stay behind and watch the mountain passes. Stuart told Robertson to keep in touch with Robert E. Lee as he moved north. Robertson was to alert Lee if the Union army started moving north in pursuit of Lee.

Those orders to Robertson may be key to the criticism Stuart's image has suffered since 1863. While Stuart took his best brigades on a raid into Pennsylvania that separated him from constant contact with Lee, he left his worst two brigades behind, under orders to stay in touch with Lee. Protecting Lee's infantry and artillery was an important role for the cavalry as Lee entered Pennsylvania, and Stuart put accomplishing that goal in the hands of the brigade commander he trusted least.

Robertson failed to accomplish most of what Stuart asked him to do during the Pennsylvania Campaign. He didn't keep in contact with Lee and didn't keep track of Union general Joseph Hooker (soon to be replaced by George Meade). Lee was in Chambersburg, Pennsylvania, before he found out the Union army was on its way to attack him. He learned of the Federals' movement north not from Stuart or Robertson but from a spy Lee was not sure he could trust.

While Stuart took the public rap for the intelligence failure at Gettysburg, he quietly passed the blame down to Robertson. Ordered out of Stuart's sight in October 1863, Robertson was sent to South Carolina, where he remained until Sherman's invasion pushed him into North Carolina. He eventually surrendered in late April 1865. He lived until 1910, some 46 years longer than Stuart.

Historians still ask the same question: Whose fault was it that Lee had to learn of the Union army's movement from a spy? Stuart was the cavalry commander whose overriding duty was to keep watch on the Federals. On the other hand, he gave specific orders to a subordinate to perform that task. It was that subordinate, Robertson, who failed to carry out the orders.

But if Stuart didn't trust Robertson, why didn't he take him along on the raid and keep an eye on him, leaving the task of screening the Federals to a more trusted brigadier? On many raids, Stuart rode with the weakest brigade commander in order to monitor his performance. But leading up to Gettysburg, he took his strongest brigades deep into Northern territory and left his weakest brigades as the closest link to Lee.

Was it Lee's fault that he didn't effectively use Robertson, Jones, or even the brigade of Albert Jenkins, who was in Pennsylvania riding scout ahead of Richard Ewell's brigade? In managing 90,000 infantrymen, Lee had more important things on his mind than taking personal command of two cavalry brigades that numbered no more than a few thousand men. Indeed, he assumed he had covered the duties of the brigades in his orders to Stuart.

Were the intelligence failures Robertson's fault? It appears that he failed to do what Stuart expected of him. Free of worry about raiding, all he had to do was guard the mountain passes and report to Lee on the location of the Federal army when Lee started moving north.

While Stuart is still the center of debate about his actions during the Pennsylvania Campaign, a case can be made that the person who bears the real fault for Lee's blindness rests in a quiet country cemetery near Blackstone.

Yellow Tavern

Yellow Tavern is located near the intersection of I-295 and US 1 north of Richmond. Virginia Center Parkway is on the right just north of the intersection. Drive down the parkway to Telegraph Road, turn right, and proceed 0.2 mile to the obelisk on the right.

Yellow Tavern, the place where one of the South's favorite heroes was mortally wounded, is a good example of how historical preservation is a relatively new concept. The battlefield is now a nondescript housing development. The only thing that memorializes the action here is an obelisk resting in a tiny plot determined by survivors of the battle to be where Stuart was shot. Houses occupy the rest of the battlefield.

When Stuart learned on May 9, 1864, that Union general Phil Sheridan was bypassing the ongoing Battle of Spotsylvania Court House and heading toward Richmond with more than 10,000 cavalrymen, he

The site where Stuart was mortally wounded

had no choice but to shadow him with his 3,000 men. Stuart was under the impression that Sheridan's goal was to attack Richmond, but Sheridan's real aim was to overwhelm the Confederate cavalry. He wanted to kill Stuart.

At 10 in the morning on May 11, Stuart reached the intersection of Telegraph Road and Mountain Road. He set up a defense in the path of Sheridan, who arrived just before noon. Instead of sidestepping Stuart and moving on Richmond, the Federals attacked. One of the commanders on Stuart's left wing was Captain Henry Clay Pate. Stuart had met Pate in 1856 at Black Jack, Kansas, when John Brown had captured him. Stuart had helped free Pate then. Now, Pate promised to hold his end of the line. He would die trying.

Around two that afternoon, the fighting died down, and Stuart began to believe that the Federals might be finished for the day. But at four o'clock, they came again, a mixture of dismounted men acting as infantry and cavalrymen charging their horses. Stuart rushed up and down his line of men, encouraging them. He finally stopped his horse among the First Virginia Cavalry, the first unit he had commanded back in 1861. Stuart drew his Whitney revolver and started firing at the advancing Federals. One of the dismounted Federals aimed a .44 caliber pistol at the mounted officer 15 yards away and fired. Stuart grabbed his side and reeled in the saddle, though he did not fall. Some of his men pulled him from his horse and put him in an ambulance.

As the ambulance was leaving the field, Stuart saw some of his men moving toward the rear. He shouted from the back of the ambulance, "Go back! Go back and do your duty as I have done mine, and our country will be safe. Go back! Go back! I would rather die than be whipped!"

While the ambulance was making its way toward Richmond, someone offered Stuart whiskey to ease the pain. He turned it down, citing the pledge he had made to his mother while still a child that he would never touch liquor. But his discomfort was such that he eventually did take a drink.

Ashland/Studley/Old Church Tavern

Stuart's three-day Ride Around McClellan in June 1862 stretched more than 80 miles on roads that still exist today. If you wish to retrace the exact route, consult the Summer 1998 issue of Blue & Gray *magazine; you should also get detailed county maps for the areas north and east of Richmond. Much of the route follows gravel rural roads through countryside that looks much like it did in 1862.*

This chapter points out a few interesting places on the ride but does not trace the route. Ashland is located along US 1 about 10 miles north of Richmond. Studley lies about 15 miles southeast of Ashland at the junction of CR 615

Stuart's ride started at what is now a shopping mall near the corner of Brook Road (US 1) and Azalea Avenue about 3.5 miles north of downtown Richmond.

The men spent the first night of the ride on a farm north of Ashland, just off US 1 near the intersection of Ellet's Crossing Road (CR 641) and Hickory Hill Road (CR 646). A historical marker stands nearby today.

Also on the route was Studley, known as Haw's Shop during the war. It is located about 15 miles southeast of Ashland, east of Hanover Court House at the intersection of CR 644 and CR 606. A Virginia Civil War Trails sign describes the action that took place in the area. Interestingly, on May 28, 1864, just two weeks after Stuart was mortally wounded at Yellow Tavern, the man who shot him, Private John Huff of the Fifth Michigan Cavalry, was mortally wounded at Haw's Shop. Wounding Stuart might have been the only thing of value Huff did during the war. He was 48 in 1864, well past his fighting prime. Records show that he spent most of

*Brook Road where Stuart started his
Ride Around McClellan*

*A farm near Ashland where Stuart's brigade
spent the first night of their Ride Around
McClellan*

his service time from 1861 until early 1864 in the hospital. Yellow
Tavern may have been his first and only real battle before he died
here.

Though the site is not on the route of the Ride Around
McClellan, it is worth noting that the remains of the only man
killed on the raid lie nearby. About 2.5 miles north of Studley on
River Road (CR 605) near the intersection with CR 644 is a large
white house under some big trees surrounded by a rail fence. Buried here in a private cemetery is Captain William Latané. Prints of
a painting of Latané's body being lowered into his grave by women
and slaves decorated Southern homes for decades after the war.
Latané received his fatal wound at what was then called Linney's
Corner, now a residential neighborhood at the intersection of

Gravesite of William Latané

Much of Stuart's Ride Around McClellan took place on Hickory Hill Road.

CR 606 and CR 634. Reports say that he was 15 paces in front of his men charging a group of Federals when he was shot.

Southeast of Linney's Corner after 1.4 miles on CR 606 is Old Church Tavern, where Stuart came to the decision to make this a true ride around McClellan. That decision might have been against orders. Lee's instructions were very specific, even though written in his maddening, loosely interpretive style. Lee told Stuart that he should not endanger his command. The orders instructed Stuart to find out what Lee wanted to know—the disposition of the Federals on the north side of the Chickahominy River—and then

Much of Stuart's Ride Around McClellan paralleled the Pamunkey River.

to return to Richmond. Stuart chose to continue the ride to see what else he could find out about McClellan. A historical marker stands at Old Church Tavern today.

The rest of Stuart's ride took him to Garlick's Landing on the Pamunkey River, to Tunstall's Station on the York River Railroad, over the Chickahominy River, and then to Charles City Court House on what is now VA 5, which parallels the James River. From there, he left his men and rode ahead to report to Lee's headquarters at the Dabbs House on the outskirts of Richmond.

The depot at Beaver Dam Station
PHOTO COURTESY OF LARRY Z. DAILY

Beaver Dam Station

Beaver Dam Station is located at the intersection of CR 652 and CR 715 northwest of Richmond. The rail station is probably not the one that stood in Stuart's day. The home called Beaver Dam still exists, but it is privately owned and is not visible from the road.

Beaver Dam Station was an important target for the Union army, as it was one of Lee's supply bases. In fact, a Union raiding party arrived here on the night of May 9, 1864, a day before Stuart passed through on his way to defend Richmond from an expected attack by Union general Phil Sheridan's forces.

Stuart met with his wife, Flora, at Beaver Dam, the nearby plantation of the Fontaine family, on May 10. It was one year since the death of his friend Stonewall Jackson. Stuart must have sensed how dangerous the next two days would be, but his actions in the presence of Flora are curious. He had always found time to visit with lady friends even while deep within enemy lines, but at Beaver Dam, he did not get off his horse to embrace his wife. He stayed mounted, bending down to kiss her after a few private words that no one was close enough to record.

Riding back to the station, where he had left his men, Stuart soberly mentioned to one of his aides that he didn't expect to survive the war. He also said he didn't want to live if the Confederacy lost. Stuart had already extracted a promise from Flora and had put it in his will that his children would be raised and educated south of the Mason-Dixon line should he die in battle.

That was the last time the couple ever saw each other. Flora received a telegram at Beaver Dam Station at noon on May 12, nearly 20 hours after Stuart's wounding at Yellow Tavern. She left immediately for Richmond, but torn-up rail lines and bridges prevented her from reaching her husband's side until four hours after his death that evening.

Evelynton Heights
PHOTO COURTESY OF EVELYNTON PLANTATION

Evelynton Heights/Berkeley Plantation

Evelynton and Berkeley are neighboring plantations on the James River. They are located on VA 5 approximately 15 miles east of downtown Richmond. Both are open to the public. For information on Evelynton, call 800-473-5075; for information on Berkeley, call 804-829-6018.

While some historians still blame Stuart for contributing to the Confederate loss at Gettysburg in July 1863, it was at Evelynton Heights in July 1862 that he actually made a larger mistake. Had Stuart thought more carefully about winning the final battle of the Seven Days' Campaign, the Army of Northern Virginia might have trapped—and destroyed—the Army of the Potomac on the banks of the James. If his principal army had been crushed just a year into the conflict, Lincoln might have been forced to end the war on the South's terms.

The Battle of Malvern Hill took place on July 1, 1862. Union

Berkeley Plantation

general George McClellan pulled his entire army back toward Harrison's Landing on the James River the next day. Berkeley Plantation, a historic home that predates the American Revolution, is located at the landing.

Lee, his army badly mauled at Malvern Hill, did not know where McClellan had gone. That night, Major John Pelham, Stuart's artillery commander, sent word that he had found McClellan at Harrison's Landing. Pelham also reported that he believed the Confederates could capture Evelynton Heights, a slight ridge that looked down on Harrison's Landing, which would give the Confederates the high-ground advantage.

The next morning, July 3, the bulk of Stuart's cavalry arrived and quickly frightened away the small force of Union cavalry that held the heights. That was a mistake. The closest Confederate infantry was at least 10 miles away, which meant at least three to five hours of marching time. By sending the Union cavalry packing, Stuart had warned the rest of the Federals that the Confederates were close. He then made a second mistake by ordering Pelham to begin firing a single six-pounder howitzer on the Union forces crowded around Harrison's Landing. The only effect the little gun had was to direct the eyes of every officer in the Union army to the heights, at which time they realized that only a small force of

The wall of the outbuilding at Berkeley Plantation where a six-pound solid cannonball is embedded in the bricks

Confederates was there. After an hour or so, Stuart sent out scouts, who learned that the Confederate infantry was still hours away from coming to his support. Stuart packed up his little cannon and rode to that force.

By the time the Southern infantry arrived, Evelynton Heights was occupied by the Union army, whose leaders had finally realized they should have a heavy force on the high ground. Generals Stonewall Jackson and James Longstreet took one look at the heights, saw how strongly they were held, and decided they were not worth attacking. Just several hours earlier—before Stuart had captured the high ground—the importance of the heights had been overlooked by the Federals.

Today, a howitzer similar to the one Pelham used is on display outside the plantation house at Evelynton Heights. At next-door Berkeley Plantation is an outbuilding with a six-pound solid cannonball embedded in the bricks. A sign there says the cannonball was fired from Evelynton Heights. If true, this might be the only known Pelham-fired artifact.

It is interesting to speculate about what might have happened had Stuart resisted the urge to attack the entire Federal army with a single, small cannon. What if he had stayed hidden, reported the vulnerability of Evelynton Heights to Jackson and Longstreet, and waited until the Confederate infantry reached his position? What would the Union officers have done if they'd looked up and seen scores of cannons and tens of thousands of muskets of the full Army of Northern Virginia—instead of a tiny howitzer and a few hundred cavalrymen armed with sabers and pistols—on the high ground above them?

Of course, there's a big what-if on the Union side, too. Could the Union gunboats on the James River have elevated their cannons to reach Evelynton Heights? If so, those large naval cannons might have wiped out Lee's army.

If Lee counseled Stuart about his rash decision to attack Evelynton Heights, he did so privately.

SOUTHWESTERN VIRGINIA

Laurel Hill

Laurel Hill is located about seven miles west of Stuart near the community of Ararat. From Stuart, drive west on VA 8, then turn right on VA 103, then right on CR 773. From Mount Airy, North Carolina, drive seven miles northeast on NC 104, which becomes CR 773 at the state line. A state historical marker denotes the site of Laurel Hill, which is administered by the J. E. B. Stuart Birthplace Preservation Trust. For more information, call 276-251-1833 or visit www.jebstuart.org.

Entrance to Laurel Hill, Stuart's birthplace

Just as his commander, General Robert E. Lee, talked about buying his birthplace, Stratford Hall east of Fredericksburg, Stuart wanted to come back to his homeplace, Laurel Hill, to live after the war. And like Lee, Stuart never fulfilled his dream.

It was at Laurel Hill that the young Stuart began to form his character. Surviving letters describe his father, Archibald, as full of "wonderful wit and humor" and "the center of attraction at every social gathering." Reading these descriptions, it is easy to see where young James (who was not called J. E. B. until his West Point years) got his personality. It was also at Laurel Hill that James's mother made him swear he would never touch liquor, apparently after she saw her husband using it too liberally.

Stuart left home as a boy to attend college preparatory school in Wytheville, then Emory & Henry College, then the United States Military Academy. He never returned home to live, though he did stop by on furlough from West Point. In 1863, Stuart wrote one of his older brothers, "I would give anything to make a pilgrimage to the old place, and when the war is over quietly spend the rest of my days there."

There is no boyhood home to see at Laurel Hill. The house burned to the ground in the winter of 1847-48, about two years after the 12-year-old Stuart went to Wytheville to live with his

The hill where Stuart's birthplace once stood

brother and start his formal schooling. His father continued to live in an outbuilding on the property. The main house was never reconstructed. The property was subsequently passed down via wills and family arrangements through J. E. B.'s mother, Elizabeth Letcher Stuart.

What is here is a 75-acre site owned by the J. E. B. Stuart Birthplace Preservation Trust, created in 1991 to preserve Laurel Hill. There are no surviving photos or engravings of the house in which Stuart was born on February 6, 1833, the seventh child and youngest surviving son of the family. According to descriptions, it was a simple wooden farmhouse, as would be expected, since Archibald Stuart was a lawyer just starting his practice in rural Virginia. Archaeological digs have established the foundations of the house and the outbuildings.

Saltville

Saltville is a valley town in southwestern Virginia. It is located eight miles north of Exit 35 off I-81 at the intersection of VA 107 and VA 42/VA 91.

Gravesite of Stuart's father, Archibald

Gravesite of Stuart's mother, Elizabeth

Gravesite of Stuart's brother, William Alexander

Nature made Saltville important because of the vast mineral deposits beneath the town. The salt was "mined" by drawing water up by pumps, then boiling the water off. The salt was packed into barrels and shipped all over the South, where it was used to preserve food for the winter. Saltville was the object of several Federal raids during the war, as the Union high command turned to a campaign of destroying the South's ability to feed its armies and civilians.

To see the graves of Archibald and Elizabeth Stuart, J. E. B.'s parents, drive northeast on VA 91 from its intersection with VA 107 in Saltville. Elizabeth Cemetery is on the left after about a mile. You can leave your vehicle in the school parking lot. Watch for two obelisks behind the small cannon at the front of the cemetery. Here rest J. E. B.'s parents. Or at least Archibald Stuart is supposed to be here. He was originally buried at Laurel Hill—the family homestead, located about 60 miles away—but was reportedly moved here to rest with his wife. Also buried here is William Alexander Stuart, J. E. B.'s older brother by six years. William never served in the war, as his work managing the

The cabin where Flora Stuart lived and taught after J. E. B.'s death

saltworks made him much more valuable here than he would have been on any battlefield.

To see another Stuart-related site, drive southwest through town on VA 91. After passing a small museum on the right, watch on the left for Stuart Drive. Turn onto Stuart Drive to see the 1795 cabin that became home for J. E. B.'s wife, Flora, after he was killed in May 1864. Flora lived with her children in half the cabin and started a school with her sister in the other half. She turned out to be a very good schoolteacher. Eventually, she moved to Staunton, where she became headmistress at what is now Stuart Hall, a preparatory school for young women.

Emory/Abingdon/GladeSpring

The village of Emory, home to Emory & Henry College, is located just north of Abingdon near Exit 26 off I-81. The graves of two men associated with Stuart are located nearby along the I-81 corridor—at Abingdon and at Glade Spring, which lies just northeast of Emory.

Collins House, the original president's house that was on the Emory & Henry College campus when Stuart attended

Stuart's first school of higher education was Emory & Henry College, founded in 1836 as a Methodist college. He entered school in 1848 at the age of 15 after attending college preparatory classes in Wytheville.

While the campus retains an old look, few of the buildings from Stuart's two years here are still in use. His dormitory, Fulton Hall, was replaced in the 1950s by Hillman Hall, located on the same site. Wiley Hall has replaced the building where Stuart took classes. Collins House, the original president's home, still stands. It is likely that Stuart was invited here on occasion, as the president regularly entertained students.

While at Emory & Henry, Stuart apparently stayed true to his pledge to his mother to avoid alcohol, though letters home hint that he sometimes got into scrapes with classmates. He once engaged in a fistfight just before an exam and spent more time trying to stop his nose from bleeding than he did on the test.

Though Stuart received a college-level liberal-arts education here, he seems to have considered Emory & Henry as something of a preparatory school. He wanted to go on to a higher college or find a lawyer who would help him "read" law.

Stuart's religious conversion at Emory & Henry marked him for the rest of his life. The details of his adoption of Methodism have been forgotten, but once he arrived at West Point in the summer of 1850, he began writing letters to friends describing how the religion he found at Emory & Henry had changed his outlook. He wrote that, while it might seem that a life in the military was a strange choice for a religious man, he felt comfortable that "a Savior's pardoning love" would protect him and "deliver me from temptation." He wrote in one letter from West Point, "Since I came here I have been more than ever satisfied of the absolute importance of an acquaintance with the Lord." Though Stuart later switched his religious affiliation to the Episcopal church, the religious fervor he developed at this small college remained with him.

A curious thing befell Stuart during his second year at Emory & Henry. Archibald Stuart, his father, ran for the United States Congress and lost. The man who beat him promptly appointed young James Ewell Brown Stuart to West Point. Family tradition holds that Stuart's appointment was the congressman's very first act in his new office. Perhaps he had been charmed by Archibald Stuart's graciousness in defeat or his fairness in running a campaign. Records do not indicate whether the new congressman met the 17-year-old before he was appointed to West Point. Stuart dropped *James* upon entering West Point and adopted the now-familiar *J. E. B.* or *Jeb*.

If you care to make a brief side trip to the grave of Stuart's biographer, head south on I-81 to Abingdon, located at Exit 17 near the Tennessee border. From Main Street in the downtown area, turn north onto US 58 Alternate. Almost immediately, turn left into Sinking Springs Cemetery. Turn right inside the cemetery and follow the dirt road leading past the Confederate section, located on the right. Directly across from the Confederate section is the grave of General John Floyd. Continue circling the cemetery on the dirt road. When you reach a point almost opposite Floyd's grave, stop, walk into the cemetery, and look for the grave of Lieutenant Colonel W. W. Blackford.

For much of the war, Blackford was Stuart's adjutant, which means that he served as a personal secretary and order writer. His role gave him constant access to the general and eventually led to the writing of his memoirs for his family at the end of the 19th century. It took another 50 years before *War Years with J. E. B. Stuart* was actually published. The book remains one of the primary sources on Stuart's character and actions. It is through Blackford's book and a similar one by another adjutant, H. B. McClellan, that the legend of Stuart as a rollicking cavalier emerged after the war.

The graves of General William E. "Grumble" Jones and his wife, Eliza, lie just a few miles northeast of Emory. Take Exit 29 off I-81, turn south on US 11, and drive 0.2 mile to Glade Spring Presbyterian Church. Directly behind the church are an obelisk and a smaller tombstone.

The gravesite of W.W. Blackford, who became Stuart's biographer

The gravesite of William E. "Grumble" Jones and his wife Eliza

One of the myths surrounding Stuart is that everyone in the South loved him. Actually, he had troubles with several of his own generals.

If there were ever two oil-and-water personalities, they were rollicking but religious J. E. B. Stuart and dour, profane William E. "Grumble" Jones. The two had similar backgrounds. Both men came from relatively modest means in southwestern Virginia. Jones even blazed the way for Stuart by attending Emory & Henry College, then getting an appointment to the United States Military Academy. Jones graduated from West Point in 1848, ranking 10th in a class of 38. Like Stuart, Jones was sent west to fight Indians. Both served in Texas for a time. Jones resigned from the army in 1857 and returned to Virginia to farm, at about the same time Stuart's career fighting Indians in Kansas was heating up.

Jones took an almost instant dislike to Stuart when he rode into Stuart's cavalry camp at Bunker Hill, Virginia (now West Virginia), in June 1861. Jones arrived as captain of the Washington Mounted Rifles, a cavalry company raised around Abingdon. Stuart had already received an appointment as lieutenant colonel. That appointment as a superior officer may have been what riled Jones. Jones, nine years older than Stuart and six years ahead of him at West Point, was two grades below Stuart in rank. It was probably no secret to Jones that John Letcher, Stuart's great-uncle, was governor of Virginia. Jones probably thought Stuart had been given rank because of who he knew, not what he knew.

"He [Jones] regarded our Colonel with intense jealousy when placed under his command, a feeling which ripened afterwards into genuine hatred as I ever remember to have seen in my experience in life," wrote W. W. Blackford in *War Years with J. E. B. Stuart*. Blackford had helped organize Jones's cavalry unit but eagerly left Jones to become "a Stuart man."

Jones actually served Stuart well during their uneasy time together. It was Jones's brigade's stubborn defense of Beverly Ford at the Battle of Brandy Station in June 1863 that saved Stuart from almost certain defeat, and maybe even capture or death.

Nonetheless, Stuart didn't like having Jones around him. He left Jones's and Beverly Robertson's brigades behind to guard the mountain passes when he took the rest of the Confederate cavalry into Pennsylvania in June 1863. Defenders of Stuart blame Jones and Robertson for Lee's being unaware of the movement of the Union army north of the Potomac, a state of affairs that eventually led to the Battle of Gettysburg. In his defense, Jones fought several sharp skirmishes with the Federals behind Confederate lines both on the way to Gettysburg and in covering Lee's retreat into Virginia, though it also appears he did not stick as close to Lee as he should have.

In October 1863, Stuart discovered that his skills had been attacked by Jones in writing. Stuart took the opportunity to court-martial Jones for insubordination. Jones kept his rank thanks to Robert E. Lee's intervention, but he agreed to be transferred back to southwestern Virginia and out of Stuart's sight. Lee's role in keeping Jones in the army may say something important. Some historians have questioned why Lee did not order Jones to follow him more closely during the Pennsylvania Campaign, the implication being that Lee's lack of information about Union army movements was as much his own fault as it was Stuart's, Jones's, or Robertson's. Perhaps Lee soothed his conscience by allowing Jones to keep his rank and his command.

Acting independently of "Whippersnapper" Stuart (as he once called his commander) was just the ticket for Jones. While operating in the upper Shenandoah Valley and in eastern Tennessee, Jones performed well at several battles, including General James

Longstreet's invasion of Tennessee in late 1863. He returned to the Shenandoah Valley in 1864. In the heat of fighting at the Battle of Piedmont on June 5 of that year, Jones was killed. It was barely three weeks after his nemesis, Stuart, had been mortally wounded.

The origin of Jones's nickname is obscure, but legend ties it to the sad story told on his wife's tombstone. On their way to Texas for one of Jones's army postings, the ship on which he and his new wife were sailing ran aground. Eliza Jones drowned when their lifeboat flipped. Her lengthy tombstone inscription reads in part, "The early death of so hopeful a sister, child and wife left her friends, parents, and husband an unspeakable sorrow." After losing the only love of his life, Jones apparently became an angry man who didn't enjoy being around laughing, joshing, singing, happy men like Stuart.

While his wife's tombstone is a virtual biography of her short life, Jones's marker does not go into detail on his career, other than saying he was a Confederate general who was "killed at the Battle of Piedmont."

Harpers Ferry sits on a triangle of land formed by the confluence of the Potomac and Shenandoah Rivers.

Harpers Ferry/Leetown

Harpers Ferry is located off US 340 about six miles northeast of Charles Town. The town's core is Harpers Ferry National Historical Park, which is open every day but Thanksgiving, Christmas, and New Year's. An admission fee is charged. Call 305-535-6298 for more information.

Leetown is about nine miles southwest of Harpers Ferry, just east of I-81 and US 11.

Harpers Ferry is a terrible place to defend. It sits on a triangle of land between West Virginia and Maryland formed by the confluence of the Potomac and Shenandoah Rivers. The town is at the mercy of any enemy that gains control of the tall ridges surrounding it.

John Brown never thought about the military complications of doing battle at Harpers Ferry when he decided to launch his slave revolt here on October 16, 1859. All he saw was that Harpers Ferry was near a free state, Pennsylvania. He imagined that fit slaves joining his revolt would send young, old, and infirm slaves through the hills surrounding Harpers Ferry to the free states. He believed his revolt would grow too large to stop.

Lieutenant J. E. B. Stuart was visiting the War Department in Washington when he learned of the revolt. He had never been to Harpers Ferry. Stuart volunteered to fetch Lieutenant Colonel Robert E. Lee, then on leave at Arlington, his home across the Potomac River from Washington. When the two officers returned to the War Department, they were ordered to board a special train to Harpers Ferry to take charge of whatever troops could be mustered to control the situation.

Stuart and Lee arrived in the town at 10 that night. Lee took charge of a 90-man detachment of marines and a group of militia. He and Stuart set up a makeshift headquarters at the head armorer's house (now the United States Park Service Information Center). Much to their relief, they saw that panicky civilians had greatly exaggerated what was happening. In Washington, the raid had been described as a vast uprising with hundreds of slaves running away from their plantations and converging on Harpers Ferry to create an army. That was exactly what John Brown hoped would happen, but in reality, the only slaves who joined him and his 21 hand-picked raiders were forced to do so at gunpoint. The slaves looked at the wild-eyed, white-bearded, screaming Brown and saw a crazy man, rather than a rescuer.

Lee's job was not to fight a slave army, as he had feared, but to rout the insurgents from the town's firehouse, where they had retreated when the townspeople began to fight back. Luckily for Lee, the raiders had chosen one of the least defensible buildings on the armory grounds. The only windows in the firehouse were higher than a man's head. Instead of choosing a building from which they could observe the soldiers or one filled with weapons and ammunition, Brown and his men had selected a small structure where they were virtually tripping over each other.

Lee waited all night before attempting to dislodge the still-unknown force. At 6:30 in the morning on October 18, Stuart voluntarily approached with a white flag in his hand. Hidden behind him was a team of 12 marines ready to storm the engine house. Stuart strode to the door and knocked, announcing that he had a message for the leader.

The door opened a crack, and Stuart found himself looking down the barrel of a Sharps rifle. When Stuart took his eyes off the weapon, he raised them to the face of the raid's leader, who had

The firehouse where John Brown and his followers were captured

been calling himself Mr. Smith in shouts back and forth during fruitless negotiations. Stuart recognized that Mr. Smith was really Mr. Brown. He had met and disarmed John Brown three years earlier at Black Jack, Kansas, while serving as part of a force that tried to keep the peace between pro- and anti-slavery forces. If Brown recognized Stuart, he didn't mention it.

Stuart read a prepared message from Lee that ordered the insurgents to surrender unconditionally. Brown didn't seem to hear. He told Stuart he would let the hostages go if he and his men were allowed safe passage back into Maryland. Stuart replied that unconditional surrender precluded any such terms. Brown insisted that the two of them strike a deal.

Realizing he was getting nowhere, Stuart waved his hat, a predetermined signal for the marines to attack. They smashed at the doors first with large hammers and then with a wooden ladder until they broke a hole in one door. One marine crawled through the hole and slashed at Brown before opening the door for the rest of the force. Two of Brown's men were bayoneted to death, Lee having ordered the marines not to load their muskets, out of fear of hitting the hostages. The whole engagement lasted just a few minutes.

Once Brown was tied up, Stuart told Lee who they had in custody. Upon learning where Brown had been staying, Stuart went to the Kennedy Farmhouse in Maryland, where he found a cache of pikes and a raft of documents implicating six wealthy New Englanders with financing Brown's plan.

Stuart's discovery of the cache of letters created a national stir for revealing "the Secret Six," Brown's financial backers. It also inflamed tensions between North and South. For years, Southerners had been claiming that the North wanted to foment slave revolts, and here was written proof. Harpers Ferry proved to them that not only did the North want a slave revolt, it wanted a bloody uprising, as affirmed by the cache of weapons discovered on the farm.

A few weeks after his adventure, Stuart was on his way west to fight more Indians. He considered the raid at Harpers Ferry to be a minor incident in his career. In fact, it foreshadowed the opening of the war by less that two years.

While you're in Harpers Ferry, you might be interested to learn that the home known as "The Bower" is located nearby. It's southwest of Harpers Ferry in the vicinity of Leetown. The home is private and is not visible from the road, so it is not recommended that you try to find it.

On September 28, 1862, after the Battle of Sharpsburg, Stuart made his headquarters at The Bower, a home Stephen Dandridge started building in 1805. From the accounts written by Stuart's staff officers, life at The Bower that fall was fun. Music filled the house. Dances were staged almost every night. The Dandridge daughters invited their cousins to the grounds to prove that Stuart was as dashing as the newspapers said, and that his artillery chief, John Pelham, was as attractive—and as single—as rumors described him.

Ever the flirt, Stuart liked to kiss the young women. So open was his affection that aide W. W. Blackford felt the need to kill any rumors about his boss. "Though he dearly loved to kiss a pretty girl, and the pretty girls loved to kiss him, he was as pure as they. I know this to be true, for it would have been impossible for it to have been otherwise and I not to have known it," Blackford wrote in his postwar book.

That fall at The Bower, a bizarre, short play was performed about a Pennsylvania farmer and his new bride. The bride, as depicted in shadow form behind a sheet, was Heros von Borcke, Stuart's oversized Prussian aide, who had somewhere found a dress

The Bower, where Stuart made his headquarters after the Battle of Sharpsburg

that fit him. Tears of laughter streaming down his face, Stuart grabbed von Borcke and said, "My dear old Von, if I ever could forget you as I know you on the battlefield, I will never forget you as a woman."

It was at The Bower that Stuart saw a small sorrel mare he later gave to Lee as a gift. Named Lucy Long, the horse was described as "low, easy moving and quiet" in a postwar newspaper article about Lee's war-horses. Lee often rode Lucy Long when he wanted to give the more familiar Traveller a rest. In memory of his deceased cavalry leader, he kept Lucy Long in Lexington, Virginia, during his tenure as president of Washington College.

It was from The Bower that Stuart launched his October 1862 raid that took him very close to Gettysburg.

The Boyd House, where Jackson stayed the longest he ever camped in one place

Bunker Hill

Bunker Hill is about eight miles south of Martinsburg on US 11 in far eastern West Virginia. Look for a Civil War monument beside the dirt lane on the south side of the community that leads to the Boyd House. The Boyd House is a private residence; do not trespass.

Records are unclear as to where Colonel Stuart set up his headquarters in mid-May 1861, other than that it was in the little "valley" community of Bunker Hill. He had barely been out of the United States Army for a week when he reported to Harpers Ferry to help consolidate and train the cavalry that would be assigned to Colonel Thomas J. Jackson's First Virginia Brigade. The two men, separated in age by nearly nine years, had never met, since Stuart had graduated from West Point three years after Jackson left the United States Army for his professor's position at Virginia Military Institute.

Within two weeks, General Joseph Johnston arrived to take overall command. Johnston immediately moved the army out of

Harpers Ferry after determining it was indefensible. He established the headquarters at Bunker Hill, located along the Valley Turnpike at the bottom—or north—end of the Shenandoah Valley.

As would be the case throughout his career, Stuart irritated someone almost immediately after he arrived on the scene. He angered Captain Turner Ashby, who had raised his own militia cavalry company from the area before the war. He also angered Captain William E. "Grumble" Jones, an older West Point graduate who had just as much Indian-fighting experience as Stuart. Ashby and Jones both wondered why the Confederate high command had taken to this brash, bearded dandy who had not even raised his own company, as they had. Stuart had done nothing to prove himself, yet he outranked them, and they were supposed to report to him. Jackson solved part of the problem by giving Ashby an independent command and assigning him to guard the Potomac River crossings. Jones had to stay. He never did warm to Stuart.

Stuart believed in on-the-job training. The cavalry camp at Bunker Hill was in disputed territory between Confederate-held Winchester and Federal-held Martinsburg. Every chance Stuart got, he sent his command toward the Federal towns to check their strength and the abilities of his officers to command their men. On occasion, Stuart exposed his forces to enemy patrols to teach them how to react to gunfire and how to properly retreat and advance.

There is an amusing story tied to the Boyd House. Following the Battle of Sharpsburg, Stonewall Jackson set up his headquarters camp in the yard of the home. He remained for more than three weeks, into October 1862. It was the longest Jackson ever stayed in one place.

One night, Stuart arrived at the camp long after everyone had retired. He slipped into Jackson's tent and lay down on the general's cot with him. This "spooning" was common behavior among soldiers during the war, when sharing body heat was the best way to stay warm on chilly nights.

Stuart slept in the next morning. When he finally arose, he walked out of Jackson's tent and saw the stern general standing by a campfire.

"Good morning, General Jackson! How are you?" the ever-loud Stuart boomed.

Jackson, who supposedly didn't have a humorous bone in his body, looked at Stuart without breaking a smile. "General Stuart, I'm always glad to see you here. You might select better hours sometimes, but I'm always glad to have you. But, General, you must not get into my bed with your boots and spurs on and ride me around like a cavalry horse all night."

No one threw a joke at Stuart without his plotting to return the favor, even if the victim was a superior officer.

Within a week or so, Stuart had guessed at Jackson's measurements and had a fine lieutenant general's coat made in Richmond. While Stuart was on a raid to Chambersburg, Pennsylvania, an aide, Heros von Borcke, delivered the coat to Jackson at the Boyd House. Jackson thanked von Borcke for the coat, then folded it, telling him that he would take good care of it. Von Borcke demanded that Jackson try it on, so he could report back to Stuart on how well it fit. Soldiers from all over camp rushed to the tent to catch the sight of Jackson giving an impromptu fashion show.

It was this coat in which Jackson posed for the famous profile photograph made just two weeks before his death.

Falling Waters

Falling Waters is located about 10 miles north of Martinsburg on US 11. The Potomac River makes a bend to the west here. The ford at Falling Waters was recognized by both sides. Though unmarked today, the battlefield likely began at the road signs announcing the unincorporated community.

The little community of Falling Waters was where two of the most famous Confederates of the war first saw action. On July 1, 1861, several thousand Union soldiers under General Robert Patterson crossed the Potomac at Falling Waters on a reconnaissance mission toward Martinsburg. Colonel J. E. B. Stuart's pickets easily discovered the movement of the slow-marching infantry. Stuart reported the news to his boss, Colonel Thomas J. Jackson, who secured permission to advance an infantry brigade <u>from</u> Martinsburg. Jackson was under strict orders to avoid a general engagement. Rather, his purpose was to discover the strength of Patterson's incursion across the river.

Considerably outnumbered, Jackson fought a slow retreat back toward Martinsburg. Eventually, the Federals grew leery that they were being drawn into a trap, so they broke off the fight. Jackson had technically lost his first battle, since he left the Federals in command of the field at Falling Waters, but the Federals actually lost more men.

Stuart performed his role as a cavalryman by the book, harassing the Federal flanks and keeping watch on where those positions were in relation to Jackson's flanks. At one point, Stuart became separated from his command. Riding alone, he came out of some woods and upon nearly 50 Federal soldiers on the other side of a rail fence. Too close to avoid being spotted, Stuart decided to act aggressively. Riding up to the Federals, he commanded them to take down the fence. The soldiers were following that order when it dawned on them that the officer did not appear to be wearing the right uniform. They were about to jump Stuart when his own command rode up and shot down three Federals reaching for their muskets.

Over the next two weeks, Stuart patrolled from Bunker Hill to Falling Waters as Confederate general Joseph E. Johnston made plans to move his army toward Manassas, where it was expected a major engagement would occur. Stuart did such a good job of keeping Patterson busy that Johnston's entire 11,000-man army boarded trains and moved to Manassas without being detected. Though he didn't have specific orders to leave the valley, Stuart led the 300 or so cavalrymen in his command toward Manassas. If there was going to be a great battle, he wanted to play a great role in it.

Maryland

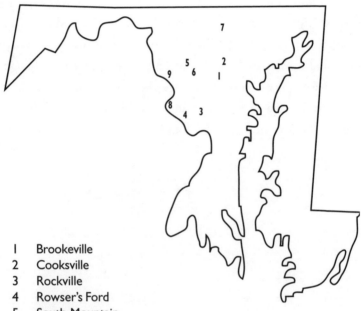

White's Ford

MARYLAND

White's Ford

> To reach White's Ford on the Potomac River, you'll need to take a short walk. First, drive two miles north from Beallsville on MD 28. Turn left on Martinsburg Road and drive another two miles, past a large power plant. Look on the right for the entrance to Dickerson Park, where you can leave your vehicle. Walk about a half-mile south on the Chesapeake & Ohio Canal towpath to Marker 39.5. White's Ford stretches across to Virginia just north of the island visible in the river.

Following their October 1862 raid, Stuart's men left Emmitsburg, Maryland, on their way back south toward the Potomac. They passed through or near New Market, Hyattstown, and Barnesville, knowing the Federals would soon be closing on them. At one point, Stuart ordered his men to use only sabers if they stumbled onto Federals. He hoped they could dispatch the enemy without firing a shot and revealing their position. Gunfire would surely bring other Federals.

Arriving here at White's Ford, Fitz Lee discovered that the far shore was protected by a regiment of dug-in infantry. He unlimbered his cannons and sent word to the Virginia side of the river under a flag of truce that he would start shelling within 15 minutes unless the Federals dispersed. To his amazement, his bluff worked. The regiment ran.

As soon as the main column reached the river, Stuart ordered the men across, telling them not to even let their horses stop for a drink, as there was no time to rest. Major John Pelham of Stuart's artillery got half of his guns across and unlimbered them on the Virginia shore, in order to start shelling the Maryland shore.

W. W. Blackford, Stuart's adjutant, volunteered to stay on the Maryland side and find Stuart's rear guard. Following the sound of firing, he located the rear guard in the dense underbrush, after which he led the men to the river and the protection of Pelham's guns. Almost as soon as the last Confederate horse stepped out of the river, thousands of Federal cavalrymen arrived at White's Ford. Without orders to pursue Stuart into Virginia, they stopped at the water's edge.

What came to be called the Chambersburg Raid was over. Not a single man of the 1,800 who participated was lost to death or capture. At least 1,200 horses were captured in Pennsylvania and Maryland. Stuart had covered more than 80 miles in three days and had deeply embarrassed the entire Federal command. He wrote his wife that he thought this raid was more successful than either his Ride Around McClellan or the raid on Catlett's Station.

When Abraham Lincoln learned of the raid, he said something very telling: "When I was a boy we used to play a game—three times around and out. Stuart has been around McClellan twice. If he goes around him once more, McClellan will be out."

Actually, Lincoln did not wait for the third time. He fired McClellan within the month and replaced him with Ambrose Burnside.

Rowser's Ford

Rowser's Ford

Rowser's Ford is located at Marker 22 on the Chesapeake & Ohio Canal, which runs beside the Potomac River. It is easier to reach the ford on the Maryland side than on the Virginia side. From MD 28 at Darnestown (located five miles west of Rockville), turn south on Seneca Road. Drive about two miles, turn left on River Road (MD 190), go 0.2 mile, and turn right on Violette's Lock Road, which dead-ends at the canal. Rowser's Ford was just below the dam.

It was here on June 27, 1863, that Stuart encountered his first serious delay on the Pennsylvania Campaign, and it came in a most dramatic way.

Heavy rains earlier in the week had filled the Potomac to as much as two feet above its normal flow. After scouting nearby Edwards' and White's Fords from the Virginia side and finding them heavily defended by Union infantry, Stuart determined that he and his three brigades (numbering about 4,500 men) would have to cross at Rowser's Ford. This was normally an easy task. However, the Potomac was now more than a mile wide.

The crossing was hazardous. The men and horses were already tired from the fighting at Brandy Station, Aldie, Upperville, and Middleburg. Now, they were being asked to cross a flooded river. The area of Virginia they were departing was so war-devastated that some of the horses had not eaten any grain or oats in three days.

Because of the water depth at Rowser's Ford, Stuart determined that his artillery limbers (two-wheeled carts pulled by the same horse teams pulling the cannons) and caissons (a type of ammunition wagon pulled by separate teams of horses) could not cross without their powder getting wet. He had the men unload the ammunition chests and hand-carry the shells above their heads as they crossed the river. The cannons, limbers, and caissons often disappeared beneath the water as the horses pulled them across.

It took hours to get the men, horses, and equipment to the other side of the Potomac. It was nearly three in the morning before the column was able to move on toward Rockville. One of Stuart's men wrote, "No more difficult achievement was accomplished by the cavalry during the war."

It was now early in the morning on June 28. Finally in the North, Stuart was already behind schedule and out of touch with Lee's infantry.

Rockville/Brookeville/Cooksville

Rockville lies immediately northwest of Washington, D.C.; I-270 is the main artery through town. Brookeville is about nine miles north of Rockville on MD 97. Cooksville is 11 miles north of Brookeville at the intersection of MD 97 and MD 144.

Stuart and his 4,500 cavalrymen were a little surprised at the rousing welcome they received from the people of Rockville when they rode into downtown on June 28, 1863. Having crossed the Potomac at three o'clock that morning, the column was focused on destroying the telegraph lines leading to Washington. The Southerners were prepared for battle, but not for the kissing and hugging they received from dozens of teenage girls who attended a school near the courthouse. One of Stuart's men later described it as "a spectacle that was truly pleasing" and noted the "gaily coloured dresses, low necks, bare arms and wildernesses of braids and curls" of young women "burning with enthusiasm to welcome the Southerner."

Though it is not the structure that existed during the war, the Montgomery County Courthouse stands on the same site on Courthouse Square near where the young women welcomed Stuart's troops. A statue of a Confederate soldier is on the grounds.

Stuart's men lingered all morning in Rockville, looking for Unionists and their property. Around noon, a scout rushed to Stuart at the Prettyman House, which still stands at the corner of South Van Buren and West Jefferson; a historical marker is located outside the house. The scout brought word that a Union wagon train coming from Washington via what is now MD 28 had almost reached the center of Rockville before realizing it was

The Montgomery County Courthouse, built in 1891, replaced the structure Stuart visited in 1863.
<small>PHOTO COURTESY OF PEERLESS ROCKVILLE HISTORIC PRESERVATION, LTD.</small>

controlled by Confederates. The Confederates swooped down upon the train, capturing at least 125 wagons filled with food. The wagon train reportedly stretched nearly eight miles.

Stuart now faced a crucial decision: What was he to do with the wagons and the 400 prisoners he had captured with them? Part of the reason for Lee's invasion of the North was to gather supplies. Stuart now had a great quantity of supplies in his possession. He resolved to head north with the wagons and prisoners.

It was a decision that has dogged him for 140 years. Some historians maintain that Stuart should have abandoned the wagons in Rockville and paroled the prisoners there, so he could move swiftly in his mission of screening Lee's army. Others counter that Lee had specifically ordered Stuart to gather supplies, so abandoning the wagon train would have been against orders.

The content of the wagons may figure into what Stuart should have done with them. Many were filled with horse oats, which meant he could feed his horses nutritionally wholesome meals in a matter of minutes, rather than grazing them in the fields for hours. One Stuart defender claims that by taking the oat wagons with him, Stuart saved at least a day's worth of gazing. In other words, he might not have made Gettysburg until the afternoon of July 3 if he hadn't kept the wagons with him for the entire raid.

Few options were open to Stuart. He couldn't send the wagons into Virginia, since the Potomac was too swollen. He could have tried to hide them along the Maryland shore until the river went down, but that would have endangered the men assigned to guard them.

Stuart thus decided to keep both the wagons and his prisoners.

That evening, he moved out of Rockville, heading north along what is now MD 97 to Brookeville, where he paroled most of the prisoners. Growing concerned that the prisoners were holding him up, he discharged the remainder at Cooksville. Knowing that Stuart was in no position to enforce the rules, since he was far behind Union lines, most of the prisoners ignored the accepted conduct for parolees, which required them to pledge to be noncombatants until formally exchanged. Those men rejoined their units within hours after Stuart paroled them.

It was just north of Cooksville that Stuart's men tore up the track of the Baltimore & Ohio Railroad and ripped down the telegraph lines. But before he destroyed the telegraph lines, Stuart learned that the Army of the Potomac was chasing Lee in earnest. It finally began to dawn on him that Lee, too, was exposed. Stuart had not been adhering to the second part of his orders—that is, he had not maintained contact with Lee.

In his after-action report, written in August 1863, Stuart noted that after tearing up the railroad, he learned that "the enemy was ascertained to be moving toward Frederick City [Maryland], north-ward, and it was important for me to reach our column [Lee's main body] with as little delay as possible, to acquaint the commanding general with the nature of the enemy's movements, as well as to place with his column my cavalry force."

Union Mills Homestead

Westminster

Westminster is northwest of Baltimore and northeast of Frederick. The Union Mills Homestead is located about seven miles north of Westminster at 3311 Littlestown Pike (MD 97). Today a Carroll County park, the mill still grinds corn and wheat. For more information, call 410-848-2288.

Built in 1797, this gristmill was so important to its community that Stuart decided not to burn it to the ground when his men passed by after midnight on June 29, 1863.

The mill's owner, Andrew Shriver, boldly told Stuart that he was a Union man, though he also admitted that other members of his family fought for the Confederacy. Impressed with the man's honesty and bravery, Stuart ordered the mill protected, though he

This gristmill still grinds corn and wheat at Union Mills Homestead.

did ask the family to make as many pancakes as it could to feed his hungry men.

Within a few hours of the time Stuart's men left, the Fifth Corps of the Army of the Potomac arrived and camped on the grounds surrounding the mill.

Stuart, assigned to keep watch on the Union army and to warn Lee of its whereabouts, now had nearly 30,000 Federal infantrymen following in his footsteps.

Urbana

Urbana is about nine miles southeast of Frederick on MD 355. The Landon House, known as the Shirley Female Academy in Stuart's day, is located within the village at 3401 Urbana Pike. It is not open for tours but may be rented for meetings and parties.

After defeating Pope at Second Manassas in August 1862, Robert E. Lee and Jefferson Davis agreed that the time was right for

The Landon House once housed the Shirley Female Academy.

an invasion of the North. In part, this was meant to convince nations like England and France that the South was strong enough to stand on its own. The plan was to march through Maryland and into Pennsylvania.

Stuart's job as a cavalry commander was to provide a screen for the infantry. He crossed the Potomac at White's Ford on September 5, several days before Lee, and rode slightly east in order to set up a series of picket posts that would watch for the Federal pursuit of Lee. The Federals would be coming from Washington, where Pope had rushed after his defeat at Second Manassas.

After riding through Poolesville and Barnesville, Stuart arrived at Urbana, where he set up headquarters in the yard of a friendly citizen. He soon spied the Shirley Female Academy. The sight of the large building and visions of his young troopers strolling around the village with young women gave Stuart an idea. He called for a "Sabers and Roses Ball" to be held in honor of the Confederates coming to liberate Maryland.

Major Heros von Borcke, Stuart's Prussian aide, took it upon himself to decorate the academy with regimental flags and bunting. Stuart found a regimental band among the trailing infantry. His guest of honor was a young woman he dubbed "the New York Rebel" for her vocal pro-Southern sentiments. It must have been a welcome, unusual respite from the war. Here in Maryland—enemy territory, since the state was still in the Union—Stuart was throwing a party complete with music and decorations.

The ball had hardly begun when cannons boomed. The officers rushed from the academy. A Federal patrol was testing a Southern outpost. Within minutes, the party ended when wounded Confederates arrived. Most of the women, including the New York Rebel, did what they could to nurse the Southerners.

Two days after the ball, Urbana fell into Federal hands as the Union army moved to catch Lee.

Stuart's brief but lively party at the Shirley Female Academy increased his legend and the love his men had for him. He knew that men who faced death at every turn treasured time away from danger. He gave them those moments.

South Mountain

The town of Burkittsville is on MD 17 west of Frederick near the West Virginia border. If you follow West Main Street approximately one mile out of Burkittsville, you'll reach Gathland State Park, located at Crampton's Gap on South Mountain. A sight well worth seeing within the park is the Civil War Correspondents Memorial Arch, erected in 1896 by George Alfred Townsend, the youngest war correspondent during the conflict and a former owner of the property on which the park now stands.

In following Lee into Maryland in the late summer of 1862, Union general George McClellan needed to cross South Mountain,

The Civil War Correspondents
Memorial Arch, erected in 1896
by George Alfred Townsend

Monument to Samuel Garland
who was killed at nearby Fox's
Gap

which meant he had to take one of several passes or roads. Lee assigned General D. H. Hill's infantry to protect most of the passes.

Stuart's cavalry was ordered to help protect the passes. Colonel Thomas Munford, who had taken over General Beverly Robertson's brigade after Robertson was transferred to North Carolina and out of Stuart's disapproving sight, saw most of the fighting here. That fighting came at the foot of Crampton's Gap, a pass just up the mountain from Burkittsville.

Stuart passed through Crampton's Gap on his way to Harpers Ferry to see if he could give Jackson a hand. Some historians have suggested that Stuart's actions indicate he didn't understand the importance of holding the gaps. Munford's cavalry brigade, even when it joined forces at the top of the gap with a brigade of infantry commanded by General Thomas Cobb, could do little to stop the Federals, who were shoving through all of the gaps at full corps strength.

The action at South Mountain led to the Battle of Sharpsburg on September 17. The cavalry did not see much action at Sharpsburg. Both armies were drawn up facing each other, which meant that Stuart had little scouting to do. Lee opted to preserve his cavalry.

Chestnut Grove

The Kennedy Farmhouse lies just across the Potomac River from Harpers Ferry, West Virginia. To reach it, take the Chestnut Grove Road exit off US 340 and drive north. The farmhouse is located at 2406 Chestnut Grove Road. A National Historic Landmark under private ownership, it is sometimes opened for those who wish to take a tour. Visit www.johnbrown.org for contact information.

After capturing and questioning John Brown and his followers at Harpers Ferry in October 1859, Lieutenant Colonel Robert E. Lee discovered that Brown maintained the headquarters of what he called his "Provisional Army of the United States" across the Potomac River in Maryland. He then dispatched Stuart and a few marines to what is now called the Kennedy Farmhouse.

Brown and his little band of followers had lived at the farm for several months, posing as cattle buyers from New York State. One of Brown's daughters and a daughter-in-law cooked for the men until just before the raid.

What Stuart found was a treasure trove of weapons and documents that sent shock waves through both North and South. Brown had amassed about 1,500 spears, or pikes, for distribution to rebelling slaves. Curiously, they were not carried along on the raid on Harpers Ferry and were never used. The letters Stuart discovered in a carpetbag in the farmhouse concerned a group of Brown's financial backers who would become known as "the Secret Six." The South saw the letters as proof that there was wide support among Northerners for a bloody slave uprising in the image of Nat Turner's revolt in 1831. The North claimed that the letters proved nothing other than that six abolitionists had given Brown expense money. The letters were used against Brown during his trial. The Secret Six feared they would be charged with financing treason against the United States. But since the war started just a year and a half later, none of them spent time in prison.

PENNSYLVANIA

Mercersburg

Mercersburg is located at the junction of PA 16, PA 75, and PA 416 about 10 miles west of Greencastle, which is just off I-81. The Steiger House, which is now a private law office, is at 120 North Main Street in Mercersburg.

Stuart's raid into Pennsylvania took place in the fall of 1862. Around noon on October 10, his men reached the town square of Mercersburg, where they set up a couple of the horse artillery's 12-pounder brass cannons to impress upon the civilians that this was a real invasion. At first, the townspeople didn't understand who the soldiers were. When it became clear that Stuart's troopers intended to confiscate local horses, some owners complained to the amused Confederates that the United States government had no power to take private property. Readily agreeing, the troopers suggested that the farmers complain directly to President Lincoln.

Stuart adjutant W. W. Blackford learned from an informant that a map hanging on a wall of the Steiger House detailed the precise location of every farm in the county. Blackford went into the house and took the map. Using it as a guide, Stuart fanned his men out to collect the horses he knew would be on the farms. The same rain that had chilled his men for hours now seemed a godsend, as it sent the farmers' horses into the barns and corrals marked on the map. Stuart particularly prized the draft horses, which were well suited for hauling his cannons.

Stuart did not use the inside of the Steiger House as his head-quarters, since the family's children had the measles. He did ask the lady of the house to fix him and his staff a meal, which they ate on the side porch.

Stuart stayed in Mercersburg only a few hours. As instructed by orders, he took some prisoners. For example, he captured the postmaster at his home, located at the northeastern corner of what is now the PA 75/PA 995 intersection. The prisoners were returned to their homes within a few weeks. Other than that, Mercersburg was left unscathed, as Robert E. Lee insisted that private property be preserved.

Chambersburg/Cashtown

Chambersburg is just off I-81 at the junction of US 11 and US 30. Cashtown is about 12 miles east of Chambersburg at the intersection of Old US 30 and Orrtanna Road.

A curious statue stands in Chambersburg's town square, located just south of the intersection of US 30 and US 11. The oddly unconcerned soldier, erected to honor the service of Union men, is depicted casually resting his wrist over the muzzle of his musket. A look at the hammer of the musket reveals that it is at full cock.

A statue that honors Union soldiers stands in Chambersburg's town square.

The soldier is about to blow his hand off. An exact copy of the statue stands in a graveyard in Wilmington, North Carolina, where it honors the unknown Confederate dead. Both towns bought their statutes ready-made from a manufacturer that was careful not to use any marks that would identify the soldier as Union or Confederate.

Stuart stood in the town square in the fall of 1862. He first saw downtown Chambersburg on the morning of October 11, in response to orders Robert E. Lee had sent two days earlier instructing the cavalry to destroy a railroad bridge over Conococheague Creek. The bridge belonged to the Cumberland Valley Railroad, though Lee did not name it as such. It was located in Scotland, a village about six miles north of Chambersburg, reached today via PA 997 from Exit 20 off I-81. The modern concrete bridge parallels Main Street's crossing of the creek.

Lee's orders authorizing the raid, written less than a month after Sharpsburg, had three purposes. First, Stuart was to find out what Union general George McClellan intended to do with his army before winter. President Jefferson Davis was worried that

Richmond might be an object of attack, so Stuart needed to see if the Federals were rearming. Second, the destruction of the bridge would severely hamper the Federals' ability to move goods from farther north to McClellan's supply base near Hagerstown, Maryland. Creating a bottleneck would make the supply-hungry McClellan even more reluctant to move his army. Third, the cavalry raid would be a simple, lightning-fast poke in the eye of McClellan, who was still camped around Sharpsburg. Stuart had become famous for riding around McClellan's army on the Virginia Peninsula in June 1862. After the devastating loss of men at Sharpsburg, Lee saw the psychological boost that would result if Stuart once again embarrassed the Union army.

After addressing the destruction of the railroad bridge, Lee wrote, "Any other damage that you can inflict upon the enemy, you will also execute. You are desired to gain all information of the position, force, and probable intention of the enemy which you can. Should you meet with citizens of Pennsylvania holding state or government offices bring them with you, that they may be used as hostages, or the means of exchanges. Such persons will, of course, be treated with all the respect and consideration that circumstances

The railroad bridge that now stands where the bridge over Conococheague Creek in Scotland once stood.

will permit. Should it be in your power to supply yourself with horses, you are authorized to do so."

Stuart left his headquarters at The Bower, a house near what is now Shepherdstown, West Virginia, on October 9. With him were about 1,800 men, though Lee had specified in his orders that Stuart was to take 1,500 soldiers. By noon, Stuart reached the town square of Mercersburg, about 15 miles southwest of Chambersburg. By eight that evening, the first Confederate riders reached Chambersburg. Arriving later that night, Stuart issued orders that public property be taken and private property protected. He operated from an unnamed public building on the square and spent the night at a nearby tollhouse after instructing pickets to be watchful for any pursuing Federal cavalry.

Stuart need not have worried. Though the Confederate cavalry had been spotted crossing the Potomac, and though Pennsylvania's governor had telegraphed the secretary of war in Washington within minutes of the Confederates' arrival in Chambersburg, McClellan did not immediately pursue Stuart. He waited nearly a day and a half before even trying to mount a response.

When the citizens of Chambersburg took stock of what was happening in their town, they were mildly surprised. As promised, no private property was harmed, though government property was taken or destroyed. The politician who surrendered the town marveled at how polite the Confederates were, even asking permission to feed their horses from his cornfield and to pump water from his well. A government storehouse full of overcoats and other uniform parts provided a wealth of goods for the Confederates.

Still, while Stuart accumulated some goods, the primary objective of the raid—the destruction of the Cumberland Valley Railroad bridge—was not accomplished. For decades, historians have generally believed the bridge was not destroyed because it was made of iron. But the truth may be that the Confederates were hoodwinked.

In a postwar letter to a newspaper editor, a Confederate officer assigned to destroy the bridge maintained that "we were informed that it was iron; our axes could not cut it and it would not burn, and as we did not have the time, nor the material to blow it up, we retraced our steps."

The letter does not mention who "informed" the Confederates that the bridge was iron, but some historians believe an unnamed civilian might have put that idea into their heads.

It is entirely possible that the Conococheague Creek bridge was made of iron. Railroads had begun replacing wooden bridges with iron ones in the late 1840s. But later war reports may contradict the assumption that the bridge was iron. On June 16, 1863, during the Pennsylvania Campaign, the cavalry of Confederate general Albert Jenkins, leading the way for Richard Ewell's infantry corps, burned an unnamed wooden railroad bridge at or near Chambersburg. Reports make no mention of an iron bridge in the area. A week later, seeing that the same bridge had been rebuilt by the Federals, Jenkins tried to burn it again on his way back through town, only to find that the wood was too green to sustain a fire. It is unclear from the records whether Stuart's supposed iron bridge and Jenkins's wooden bridge were one and the same.

Adding to the confusion is a local county history that says that an iron bridge did not cross Conococheague Creek until the 1870s.

Did a simple Yankee-told lie to some tired, wet, cold Confederates lead to the bridge's being spared? Did low-ranking Confederate officers lie to their commanding officers about why they didn't destroy the bridge? Did those officers even see the bridge with their own eyes? Did General William E. "Grumble" Jones, whose brigade was assigned to destroy the bridge, confirm that it was made of iron before writing so in his report?

Did the misunderstanding or misrepresentation that the bridge was iron make it all the way up the chain of command? It appears it did. Robert E. Lee, apparently after reading Stuart's report, which was based on Jones's report, sent a letter to President Davis saying that the iron bridge could not be destroyed.

On the morning of October 10, Stuart rode east out of Chambersburg, much to the surprise of his subordinates, who had assumed they would turn west and then south. As the Confederates moved along what is now US 30 toward Cashtown, Stuart called aside his adjutant, W. W. Blackford. A puzzled Blackford reined in his horse as Stuart pulled out a topographical map.

"If I should fall before reaching Virginia, I want you to vindicate my memory," Stuart said to a speechless Blackford. He explained that he thought the Federals believed he was making an in-and-out raid. If so, they would be waiting for him in the south to return the same way he came. Instead, he was heading east to strike where the Federals least expected. Blackford noted later in his book that Stuart's eyes were misted with tears, something Blackford had never seen.

Stuart used Cashtown as a marker from which to begin the march back south. Upon reaching the village, he had his men dismount and rest for a short time. Stuart took the first nap he'd enjoyed since departing on the raid more than 36 hours earlier. Then he abruptly turned and headed for Emmitsburg, Maryland, taking the Orrtanna Road toward Fairfield.

It was while Stuart was resting at Cashtown—perhaps at the Cashtown Inn, which still exists today—that McClellan began to form what he thought was a foolproof idea to bag the Confederates. He would spread his men along the Potomac in a picket line that the Confederates would not be able to penetrate. McClellan sent a telegram to Secretary of War Edwin Stanton vowing "to teach them a lesson they will not soon forget."

McClellan's plan to stop the Confederates from recrossing the Potomac was a good one. He built a series of elevated signal stations and had telegraph operators standing by around the clock. Two full infantry divisions were loaded into railroad cars, the engines built to full steam so the troops could pull out at a moment's notice when Stuart was spotted. Eight cavalry regiments guarded every likely ford. It was as if McClellan had strung tripwires along a 50-mile front.

The plan nearly worked. At White's Ford in Maryland, Fitz Lee bluffed a Union regiment into running. Stuart then hurried his men across the Potomac into Virginia just before thousands of Federal cavalrymen arrived on the scene. He had made his escape, and the raid into Pennsylvania was at an end.

Gettysburg

Gettysburg is located in south-central Pennsylvania about 10 miles across the border from Maryland. Five different roads lead to the town; the easy accessibility that led Robert E. Lee to concentrate his army here in mid-1863 still applies today. The primary roads are US 30, US 15, PA 34, and PA 116. The visitor center at Gettysburg National Military Park lies south of town. Admission to the park is free; call 717-334-1124 for details. The East Cavalry Field, where Stuart fought on the third day of the battle, is about three miles east of downtown. It is accessible from either US 30 (York Pike) or PA 116 (Hanover Road). Stuart arrived via what is now US 30.

When Stuart reached Gettysburg, he found Lee not at his head-quarters but on Seminary Ridge surveying the scene in front of him. Accounts vary as to what Lee said. One has him looking Stuart up and down and then saying, "Well, General Stuart, you are here at last." Another account, perhaps embellished, as it was written years after the war, has Lee raising his arm, almost as if to strike Stuart, before asking, "Where have you been? I have not heard a word from you in days, and you are the eyes and ears of my army!" When Stuart explained that he had 125 wagons loaded with sup-plies, Lee replied, "They are an impediment to me now." Lee then softened his tone, pointed toward the Federals on Cemetery Ridge, and said, "Help me fight these people."

That night, the fatigued Stuart acted strangely. He first or-dered his men to remain in the saddle in case the Federals at-tacked. Finally talked out of that, he rested until the next morning. It was only then that he realized his men were low on ammuni-tion. It took hours before they had cleaned and reloaded their weap-ons and filled their cartridge boxes.

On the morning of July 3, 1863, Lee apparently gave Stuart vague verbal orders to support the Confederate left flank. Stuart, always prone to stretching things a little farther than his com-manders intended, rode with his 5,000 men about three miles east of Gettysburg on the York Pike to the general rear of the Federals on Cemetery Ridge.

Lee apparently did not intend for Stuart to try to split the Union forces from the rear if the impending Pettigrew-Pickett-Longstreet attack on the Union infantry's center succeeded. Nei-ther Stuart nor Lee knew the condition of the landscape behind the Federal lines, nor when the infantry attack would take place, as Lee had left that decision to General James Longstreet. What Lee must have hoped would happen was for Stuart to sweep in as close to the Union lines as possible and distract the Federal infantry massing on Cemetery Ridge.

When Stuart reached Cress's Ridge, he did something that still has historians scratching their heads. He fired a cannon several times in several directions at nothing in particular. He either was trying to attract Federal reinforcements from Cemetery Ridge or was signaling Lee that he was in place before the main infantry attack. The behavior was doubly strange, as Stuart had been trying to keep his presence a secret by having his men remain close to the woods.

The cavalry battle opened when Stuart pushed a brigade of newly acquired western Virginians recently under the command of General Albert Jenkins (who'd been wounded earlier in the battle and was not present on the third day) toward the Rummel Farm. Stuart hoped to use Jenkins's men as a lure to get the Federal regiments in the area to come out in the open. Once the Federals attacked Jenkins's men, Stuart would spring from the wood line with the brigades of Wade Hampton and Fitz Lee.

It was a good plan that didn't work. Jenkins's men pulled back when they ran low on ammunition, before the Federals committed themselves to any action. Fitz Lee and Wade Hampton had to come out of the wood line without the element of surprise they hoped to

A view of Rummel Farm

A Confederate cannon aimed at Rummel Farm

have. They led a saber-swinging charge similar to that at Brandy Station the previous month. The site of this action is noted by historical markers.

Union general George Custer led a countercharge, shouting to his Michiganders, "Come on, you Wolverines!" Custer should not have been there. He was part of a different cavalry division on a different part of the battlefield, miles away, when Stuart's old nemesis, Union general David Gregg, asked for his men as reinforcements. Gregg had been ordered to move away from the intersection of Hanover Road and Low Dutch Road (the southern access to the East Cavalry Field), but he suggested to his commanders that he stay where he was, as it seemed a strategic spot the Confederates would covet.

Gregg's hunch was right on target. Had he moved away as ordered, and had he not asked for Custer's help, Stuart could have easily taken the East Cavalry Field. What Stuart would have done then is impossible to tell. The Pettigrew-Pickett-Trimble Assault faded away by 1:30 that afternoon. Stuart's undermanned mounted brigades would have been unable to do anything with the triumphant Union

*A monument showing a Union cavalryman
stands guard at East Cavalry Field*

infantry forces firmly entrenched on Cemetery Ridge.

Had Lee's infantry broken the Union infantry line, however, and if those Union infantrymen had come streaming back east, Stuart's men would have been in their way. Perhaps the presence of the Confederate cavalry in the rear of the Federal infantry would have caused panic.

But that is just speculation. The reality was that for the next 10 days, Stuart was in the saddle almost constantly, covering the retreat of Lee's army back across the Potomac.

Before the hair on his horse was dry from that crossing, the formal complaints over Stuart's behavior during the Pennsylvania Campaign began. Lee's chief of staff urged for Stuart's court-martial. Lee himself wrote that "the movements of the army preceding the battle of Gettysburg had been much embarrassed by the absence of cavalry." The criticism centered on Stuart's not being close enough to Lee to keep him informed of the location of the Union army.

Stuart maintained that he had followed orders by capturing supplies and disrupting Federal communications, and that he had

*A close-up of the First
Regiment of the Maryland
Cavalry monument*

left General Beverly Robertson's and General William E.
"Grumble" Jones's brigades in Virginia to screen Lee's infantry and
keep him informed of the whereabouts of the Federals once Lee
crossed the Potomac.

All of that was true, but Robert E. Lee was still the commanding general and still had the power to discipline men he felt had
failed him. Lee disciplined his cavalry commander by ignoring
Stuart's expectation that he would be promoted to lieutenant
general.

By contrast, Gettysburg was General David Gregg's finest hour
as a cavalryman. Gregg was modest about his actions at the East
Cavalry Field, but others fully credited him with defeating Stuart.
Custer was appreciative that Gregg had asked him to fight. Had
Custer stayed with his own division, he may have been killed in
the foolhardy charge ordered by his division commander against
infantry behind a stone wall miles away from the East Cavalry Field.
Instead, while temporarily serving under Gregg, Custer became a
household name because of his successful charge in breaking up the

David Gregg's gravesite, located in Reading, Pennsylvania

Confederate cavalry line. He became famous thanks to Gregg and Stuart.

Gregg continued fighting in the East even after U. S. Grant took over in the spring of 1864 and handed command of the cavalry to Phil Sheridan. Gregg seemed to work well with Sheridan, but some of his supporters felt that his victory on the East Cavalry Field went unrewarded by his superiors.

Gregg suddenly resigned from the army in late January 1865, citing a "demand for my continued presence at home." Though he had played a major role in the rise of the Union cavalry, he never shared in the glory that went to Sheridan and Custer. Gregg lived into his 80s, thereby becoming one of the longest-surviving Civil War generals. He proved to be valuable even as an old soldier. When the East Cavalry Field was being surveyed for preservation, he personally pointed out the woods where Stuart had started his charge and his own men had launched their countercharge.

A statue of a Union cavalryman commemorates the battle that took place in Hanover, Pennsylvania.

Hanover

Hanover is located in south-central Pennsylvania at the intersection of PA 94 and PA 194 about 15 miles east of Gettysburg. Most of the fighting here took place within sight of the downtown square, where a statue of a Union cavalryman commemorates the battle. The hotel used as a headquarters by Union general Judson Kilpatrick is on the northwest corner of the square.

On June 30, 1863, the forces of Judson Kilpatrick were moving through the streets of Hanover when Stuart's men, coming up what is now PA 194, spotted them. Figuring they would be attacked in force if they waited, the Confederates pitched into the rear of the Union column close to the center of downtown. For several hours, the two sides traded fire in the streets. Artillery set up on opposing hills fired at each other.

Stuart, watching the battle from a hill south of the square, suddenly found himself in the thick of the fighting when part of his command retreated, bringing pursuing Federals with them. Stuart, mounted on one of his favorite horses, Virginia, jumped a hedge and found himself facing 30 Federals trying to flank the fleeing Confederates. He quickly realized that he and his adjutant, W. W. Blackford, were in danger. Wheeling his horse south with the rest of the fleeing cavalrymen, he could not resist calling, "Rally them, Blackford!"—meaning that he wanted his aide to stay behind and stop the Confederate rout. Of course, Blackford was too busy riding away from the pursuers to attempt any such thing. Together, the two men jumped their horses over a 15-foot ditch, which proved too wide for the Federals to try themselves.

"I shall never forget the glimpse I then saw of this beautiful animal up in mid-air over the chasm and Stuart's fine figure sitting erect in the saddle," wrote Blackford in *War Years with J. E. B. Stuart*. Once again, Stuart escaped capture by knowing how to get the most out of his horse.

The ditch was later filled in as the city grew. Historians place it on Hanover Street, three blocks southwest of the town square on the site where Hanover Elementary School sits today.

Blackford later wrote that the wagon train Stuart had captured near Rockville, Maryland, interfered with the cavalry's movements in the narrow roads leading into Hanover. He suggested that had Stuart realized how much trouble the wagons would be, he would have burned them. But since Stuart intended to meet with Jubal Early in nearby York, he clung to the wagons as prizes of war.

Stuart headed toward York but found that Early had moved to the west to meet Lee. Now, for the first time since leaving Virginia, Stuart sent a courier to tell Lee that he was nearby. Since he didn't know where Lee was, Stuart pointed his men in the direction of Carlisle, 20 miles northwest of Gettysburg. He would spend another day reaching Carlisle and shelling that town's square before he finally got a note from Lee telling him to come to Gettysburg. There is little evidence of Stuart's visit to Carlisle now.

Fort Putnam

NEW YORK

West Point

The United States Military Academy at West Point is on the west bank of the Hudson River about 40 miles north of New York City. The post is normally open for walking and bus tours. A small museum is located behind the visitor center. Call 845-938-2638 for more details about visiting.

Most of the barracks and instructional buildings that were around during Stuart's four-year career at West Point in the early to mid-1850s have long since been replaced, but the Hudson Valley still offers the same beautiful mountain scenery that reminded Stuart of his Blue Ridge roots.

Fort Putnam, a Revolutionary War fort that rises above West Point, was a favorite spot that allowed cadets a fine view of the valley. Pick up a map at the visitor center and ask if the fort is open. Its hours are irregular, but visitors are few, so you can enjoy the same solitude that the cadets sought in walks to the old stone fort.

Quarters 100

One of the two buildings that survive from Stuart's day is the superintendent's living quarters, known as Quarters 100. It faces the parade ground. This house remains in active use and is off-limits to tourists. During Stuart's tenure here, the superintendent was Robert E. Lee. Cadets often visited him in his house. Stuart mentioned in letters home to his mother that he considered Mrs. Lee to be like a second mother to him. His letters also hint that he may have been sweet on one of the Lee daughters, but he apparently never asked Lee's permission to court her. Asking the commander of the academy for permission to date his daughter would have likely been too forward for even a cadet as bold as Stuart.

The other surviving building is the Old Cadet Chapel, located outside West Point's cemetery. Stuart, a devout Methodist when he came to West Point, worshiped here. He later became an Episcopalian on the Kansas frontier.

Stuart seems to have approached West Point like he did everything else in life—with a song in his heart and on his lips. His friend Fitzhugh Lee, Superintendent Lee's nephew and later one of Stuart's most trusted brigade commanders, later wrote that Stuart had "much music in his voice" on the parade ground.

This love of a good time was not necessarily what the United

States Army expected from its future officers. Stuart regularly got demerits for being late or unkempt and for fighting. To his credit, he admitted to his parents that he had been caught fighting; they wrote letters admonishing him for his bad behavior. Other than giving him demerits, the army never punished Stuart too severely. After all, part of his schooling was to learn how to fight and when to defend his honor—or that of the nation. Nor surprisingly, one subject at which Stuart excelled was horsemanship.

While at West Point, Stuart found ways to meet members of the opposite sex, though he was not overly impressed. He once wrote, "The more I see of these Yankee girls the more thoroughly I am convinced of their inferiority in every respect to our Virginia ladies, in beauty especially."

Stuart graduated 13th in a class of 46. This was not good enough to get him an appointment in the Engineering Corps (which he didn't really want anyway) and not bad enough to get him sent to the infantry (traditionally the post of the bottom third of the class). His first duty would be patrolling for Indians in Texas with the Mounted Rifles. His dream of being a dragoon was thus met.

Gravesite of Stuart's father-in-law,
Phillip St. George Cooke

MICHIGAN

Detroit

> General Phillip St. George Cooke, Stuart's father-in-law, is buried in Elmwood Cemetery. The cemetery is located at 1200 Elmwood Avenue, which is east of the downtown area and close to the Detroit River. Cook's grave is in the right rear portion of the cemetery, designated as Section H, Lot 94; it is marked on the cemetery map available at the office.

It is not often that your son-in-law makes you out to be a fool in front of your bosses and the nation. But that is what happened when 29-year-old Confederate general J. E. B. Stuart ran rings around his 53-year-old father-in-law, Union general Phillip St. George Cooke, in June 1862.

When Stuart undertook his famous four-day ride around General George McClellan's Army of the Potomac as the Federals were massing east of Richmond, Cooke was sent after him. Not only did he fail to stop Stuart or bring him to battle, he failed to even locate him long enough to fire many shots in his direction. During Stuart's ride, which established that the northern wing of the Federals was isolated and vulnerable to attack, only one Confederate cavalryman was killed. The ride provided the intelligence needed for Lee to launch the Seven Days' Campaign, which saved Richmond from capture. It was after those events that Stuart emerged as a Southern hero.

Though Cooke led his cavalry division fairly competently during the Peninsula Campaign and the Seven Days' Campaign, McClellan didn't like the rumors circulating around the army that he had allowed his son-in-law to escape capture out of family loyalty. A humiliated Cooke was quietly eased out of duty in the East, where he might again come in contact with his son-in-law. No Union commander wanted to be associated with the father-in-law of J. E. B. Stuart.

Though Cooke was not forced entirely out of the army, it was a sad, abrupt end to a life of service just when the Union needed men like him—men who knew what they were doing.

Cooke's personal story is one of split loyalties and shattered family ties. His career story is a sad example of how quickly superiors can abandon a loyal soldier when things do not go quite right in war.

Born in Leesburg, Virginia, Cooke was appointed to West Point at the tender age of 14. He graduated in the bottom third of his class in 1827 as an 18-year-old second lieutenant, following which he had a fine prewar career on the frontier. When not fighting Indians, Cooke explored new routes for westward expansion. He led the longest military march on record, a 2,000-mile route that started in Iowa and ended at the Pacific Ocean. That carefully mapped trail marked the beginning of the first wagon road from Santa Fe, New Mexico, to California. Soldiers' accounts of his exploration of New Mexico, Arizona, Utah, and California are full of praise for Cooke for leading his men across vast deserts.

In 1855, he was in command at Fort Leavenworth, Kansas, when a new second lieutenant from Virginia reported for duty. If Cooke himself did not see promise in Lieutenant J. E. B. Stuart—nicknamed "Beauty" by his friends at West Point—Cooke's daughter Flora sure did. They were married later that year, after Cooke had been transferred to nearby Fort Riley, Kansas.

During the mid- and late 1850s, Cooke was among the most respected field-grade officers in the United States Army. He was a colonel when Robert E. Lee was a lieutenant colonel. During the Crimean War, the army thought enough of Cooke's military skills to send him to Europe to evaluate what was then considered modern warfare. He came back to write a manual on cavalry tactics that was studied by both Union and Confederate officers throughout the Civil War.

When the war came, Cooke stayed loyal to the Union, while two daughters and one son, John Rogers Cooke, became Confederates. John Rogers Cooke demonstrated that military competence ran in the family. He became one of the better brigadier generals in the Confederate army, though he was an infantry commander. Daughter Julia stayed loyal to her father's wishes and married a Union officer, Jacob Sharpe. Sharpe was later brevetted a general in the war, though he was never officially given the rank.

Stuart was so angry at his father-in-law's abandonment of Virginia that he renamed his son, who had been christened Phillip in honor of his grandfather. Stuart said this of Cooke's decision to stay with the Union: "He will regret it but once, and that will be continually." Stuart virtually forbade anyone to mention his father-in-law's name in his presence. He also daydreamed about capturing him on the field of battle. But once he humiliated Cooke during the Ride Around McClellan, the Federal high command made sure that would never happen.

McClellan, looking for any means to explain his ability to snatch defeat from the jaws of victory during the Peninsula Campaign and the Seven Days' Campaign, seized on Cooke's ties to his son-in-law. Cooke had failed to bring Stuart to battle during the Ride Around McClellan. He had also ordered a cavalry charge at Gaines Mill that resulted in nearly half a regiment's men being cut down. In the confusion, the Federals lost 22 cannons to Confederate capture, which Union general Fitz John Porter blamed on Cooke's ill-timed attack. That was good enough reason for McClellan to demand Cooke's transfer out of his command.

The charge of incompetence, particularly in his handling of cavalry, angered Cooke. Twenty years after the battle, Porter and Cooke traded written charges through articles over who was responsible for the loss of those guns. Cooke maintained that his charge had been necessary to keep the Confederates at bay. Porter claimed that panic had ensued following the charge.

At age 53 in 1862, Cooke was older than most of his fellow generals. Nonetheless, he was one of the best trained and most experienced military leaders the United States had. While it is true that he failed to stop his son-in-law and that he ordered one disastrous charge, Cooke's overall performance in the first year of the war was decent. Still, scapegoats are always needed in warfare. McClellan's demand to remove Cooke was met.

After spending months in limbo, Cooke was finally sent to Baton Rouge, Louisiana, where he spent most of his time on court-martial duty. The man who had literally written the book on cavalry tactics—the man who some called "the father of the United States Cavalry"—was ordered behind a desk because his famous son-in-law was embarrassing other Union commanders.

Such humiliation did not drive Cooke out of the army, though that was probably the aim of the Washington policy makers who approved McClellan's demand. The army quickly forgot about the man who had laid the groundwork for its eventual cavalry domination. Officially, it treated him with respect, even brevetting him with the rank of major general, but it never again turned to him for a field command. The ostracism continued even after the war, when the army pushed into western Indian lands where Cooke had pioneered for the government. Instead of using his knowledge of the land to develop a plan to operate against the Indians, the United States Army sent him to Detroit in 1870. He stayed in the army until 1873.

Even after the old soldier's retirement, the Cooke family could not mend the differences that had begun with Virginia's secession from the Union. Though he had lived in Detroit for only three years before retiring, the old general chose to spend the rest of his life in that city, rather than return to Virginia. The Sharpes stayed, too.

J. E. B. Stuart and Cooke's daughter Flora are buried in Richmond's Hollywood Cemetery, where admirers visit their graves every day. Cooke died in 1895. He, his loyal daughter Julia, and his little known son-in-law are all buried in the same plot hundreds of miles from the rest of his family. The man who started a revolution in the United States Army's mounted forces lies mostly forgotten in the back of a Detroit cemetery.

The base commander's house at Fort Leavenworth, where Flora Cooke lived

Fort Leavenworth

> Fort Leavenworth, located near the famous federal prison, is an active military post. It is off Metropolitan Avenue (US 73) just north of the town of Leavenworth in northeastern Kansas. Though this is an open post, visitors must present a photo ID and tell their destination when they reach the checkpoint.

Stuart came to Fort Leavenworth in the summer of 1855 as quartermaster for the fort. It was not long after his arrival that he noticed a pretty young woman on a spirited steed. Though he initially imagined himself rescuing her from a runaway horse, he soon noticed that she handled a mount as well as he did. He sidled up to the young woman to introduce himself. He must have gulped when the object of his affection identified herself as Flora Cooke. She was the daughter of the post commander, Colonel Phillip St. George Cooke. Flora must have been as taken with Stuart as he was with her. In September, less than two months after his arrival, Stuart proposed marriage, and Flora accepted.

You'll enter the post on Grant Avenue. If you care to visit the Frontier Army Museum, take the fourth street to the right, Reynolds Avenue. The museum is on the left at the next intersection. Though it has no artifacts directly related to Stuart, it offers excellent displays of the kinds of weapons, uniforms, saddles, and wagons he used in 1855. The museum is open seven days a week. Call 913-684-3186 for more information.

Leaving the Frontier Army Museum, turn right on Grant Avenue, drive three blocks, and turn left on Kearny Avenue just past the statue of U. S. Grant. Make an immediate right onto Sumner Place. The long building at 12-14 Sumner Place is The Rookery, the oldest house in Kansas and once the post headquarters. In his role as quartermaster, Stuart likely visited this building on occasion.

At 20-22 Sumner Place is the former post commander's headquarters, where Colonel Cooke and his family lived at the time Stuart was assigned here. Stuart called on Flora in this house, un-

The quartermaster's building where Stuart worked while at Fort Leavenworth

der the watchful—and disapproving—eye of his commander and future father-in-law. Colonel Edwin Sumner took up residence here after the Cookes moved to Fort Riley; Stuart also served under Sumner.

Across from the headquarters is the parade ground, where Stuart probably tried to dazzle Flora and her father with his horsemanship.

Fort Riley

> *Fort Riley is located outside the city of Manhattan in eastern Kansas. To reach it, take Exit 301 off I-70. Though this is an open post, security concerns dictate that everyone in the vehicle must have a photo ID and must explain their purpose in visiting the fort. Make sure you leave your visitor pass on the dashboard.*

Fort Riley is where Stuart married Flora Cooke, whom he had met at Fort Leavenworth. It is also a great place to get a sense of what cavalry life was like on the frontier.

You should begin your exploration of Fort Riley at the United States Cavalry Museum. You'll enter the fort on Holbrook Road; the museum is located at the intersection of Holbrook and Custer Avenue. Leave your vehicle along a convenient side street, preferably Sheridan Street, one block north of the museum.

The south wing of the museum, built in 1855, was used as a hospital during Stuart's time here. The museum features weapons and uniforms, including hats and footwear, used from the formation of the cavalry right through the 1930s, when it was disbanded. Of particular value to visitors trying to understand the United States

Army's tactics against the Plains Indians is a map explaining how regiments had to be split into smaller units to cover the vast territory. The museum also has an excellent display of weapons, including the standard cavalry saber, nicknamed "the Wristbreaker" because of its heft. Stuart and every other cavalryman carried a saber, a Colt revolver, and a Sharps carbine on standard patrol.

Curiously, the museum does not display the saber device Stuart invented while at Fort Riley. It allowed troopers to more quickly hook and unhook their saber scabbards from their belts to their saddles. It was while Stuart was in Washington, D.C., in October 1859 obtaining a patent for the device that he heard about John Brown's raid on Harpers Ferry. He left the War Department to fetch Robert E. Lee at his home.

Neither does the museum describe the 1857 Battle of Solomon's Fork, the first real attempt to dislodge the Plains Indians from their land and a battle in which Stuart was wounded.

The museum is open seven days a week. For more information, call 785-239-2737.

Leaving the museum, walk north to 24-A Sheridan Avenue to visit the Custer House. The home is mistakenly named, as George Armstrong Custer actually lived in a nearby house (21-A) that is

The Custer House

The parade ground at Fort Riley

still in use today. On occasion, 24-A is opened so visitors can get a sense of what it was like to inhabit officer's quarters in the 19th century.

Right across from the Custer House and beside the United States Cavalry Museum is the parade ground on which Stuart and the troopers of 1855 showed off their horses.

From the Custer House, drive west on Sheridan, then bear right when it intersects Heuber Road (KS 18). Quarters 123 is on the left almost immediately after the turn. This was the residence of the post chaplain who performed the marriage ceremony on November 14, 1855, for J. E. B. Stuart and Flora Cooke, daughter of Fort Riley's commander, Colonel Phillip St. George Cooke. The wedding may have taken place in the house, as the post chapel was not yet built. Post historians believe that United States Army colonels Joseph Johnston and Robert E. Lee, both at Fort Riley for court-martial duty, may have attended the wedding, as they would have wanted to honor the daughter of the commander. Stuart was a favorite student of Lee's at West Point. For one day in 1855, this small house may have hosted three men who would become top Confederate generals and one man who would become a discredited Union general.

St Mary's Chapel

Continue north on Heuber for another few hundred feet, then turn right onto Barry Avenue. Behind the modern, large church is the smaller, older St. Mary's Chapel. Stuart probably contributed money to build this chapel, which was under construction in 1855. It was not completed until 1857, two years after his wedding.

Baldwin City

Baldwin City is located on US 56 just south of Lawrence in eastern Kansas. From US 56 two miles east of Baldwin City, turn south onto CR E2000 and drive about half a mile to the small park on the right, where you'll see a historical marker.

While most people associate John Brown with his raid on Harpers Ferry in October 1859, he began making a name for himself in Kansas in the summer of 1856. By pure chance, Lieutenant J. E. B. Stuart met Brown at this spot in June 1856, three and a half years before encountering him again in a fire-engine house in Harpers Ferry.

The term *civil war* is misapplied to the conflict of 1861-65. By definition, it means that one faction in a country is warring against another faction to gain control of the same government. But when the South seceded from the Union, it formed its own government, created it own capital, and never expressed any interest in fighting for control of Washington, D.C.

Five years earlier, however, a real civil war was fought on American soil. *Bleeding Kansas* is more than just a descriptive term. While there are no hard figures, historians believe that the political struggle over admitting Kansas into the Union as a slave or a free state cost the lives of several hundred people. Starting in 1855, pro-slavery men from Missouri and anti-slavery men from various non-slave states poured into the Kansas Territory and tried to shape the future by claiming to be legitimate voters. While the clashes between the two sides were really organized murders rather than battles, some of them resembled the kind of skirmishes common in the Civil War.

One of these was the Battle of Black Jack, described by Kansas historians as the first battle between free and slave states. The battle came about after two dozen anti-slavery men killed five pro-slavery settlers on nearby Pottawatomie Creek. A small body of pro-slavery militia organized in Missouri to track down the killers. On June 2, 1856, the pro-slavery men caught up with the murderers in this stand of trees. For all their self-proclaimed fierceness, the pro-slavery militia quickly scattered when attacked by the anti-slave militia, which was led by John Brown, who was just becoming a recognized name in the abolition movement. Brown and his men captured some of the pro-slavers, including their leader, Henry Clay Pate.

The captured men must have feared they would suffer the same fate that had befallen the pro-slavery settlers. Brown's group had hacked men to death in front of their families using short broadswords similar to what Roman gladiators carried. Brown had killed the men, who did not actually own any slaves, in order to strike fear in the hearts of any actual slave owners who might try to move to this section of Kansas.

Three days after the Battle of Black Jack—which resulted in no deaths but some wounded on both sides—a detachment of the First United States Cavalry arrived. The cavalry was commanded by Colonel Edwin Sumner, who was assisted by Lieutenant J. E. B. Stuart. The soldiers learned that Brown still had about a dozen very nervous prisoners with him, including Pate, who was a deputy United States marshal. Under orders from President Franklin Pierce to disperse bands of armed men whether they be pro- or anti-slavery, Colonel Sumner demanded that Brown release his prisoners. Brown reluctantly complied.

Everyone but Brown seems to have missed the significance of this meeting between the United States government and what Brown considered the nucleus of his future army of liberation. In the view

The site of the Battle of Black Jack, the first battle between free and slave states

of Stuart and Sumner, they were obeying orders to disarm bands of men causing heightened tensions on the Missouri-Kansas border. But Brown saw his encounter with the cavalry as something more diabolical. He came to believe that the government had taken sides in the slavery dispute. He thought that the only means to destroy slavery in the nation would be a slave revolt against the government.

Stuart and Brown met only once in Kansas. Brown did not leave the state for several months. He took part in several other, larger skirmishes with pro-slavery forces, fights that made him a household name. Stuart stayed in Kansas another year but turned his attention to fighting Indians, rather than abolitionists.

An interesting artifact originated at the Battle of Black Jack. When Brown captured Henry Clay Pate, he took a bowie knife from the Missourian. Pate apparently forgot to retrieve the knife. Brown took it with him back to New England, where he asked a blacksmith to duplicate its long, thick blade into 1,500 copies, to be mounted on poles to make pikes. These would be used to arm Brown's envisioned army of slaves.

Three and a half years later, when Brown opened the door of the fire-engine house at Harpers Ferry in response to Stuart's demand, Stuart recognized the abolitionist immediately. If Brown recognized Stuart as the lieutenant from the Battle of Black Jack, he didn't mention it. After Brown was captured in the ensuing fight inside the fire-engine house, Stuart liberated the same bowie knife from Brown. He kept it as a souvenir. It is now on display at the Virginia Historical Society in Richmond, along with other Stuart relics.

Henry Clay Pate later joined the Confederacy and served under Stuart's command. He lost his life in the same battle in which Stuart was mortally wounded.

Morland

The site of the Battle of Solomon's Fork, the first con-
frontation between the United States Army and the Chey-
enne Indians, is one mile west of the small town of Morland,
which lies along US 24 about 12.3 miles west of its inter-
section with US 283 in northwestern Kansas. Find Morland's
Main Street and drive west on the dirt road until you cross
the bridge at the South Fork of the Solomon River. To the
right is private property that matches the description of the
battlefield and on which artifacts such as musket balls have
been found. Also on the property is what appears to be the
site of the sod fort inside which Stuart rested after his wound-
ing. Although efforts are under way to recognize the site, no
marker stands here at present.

Providence sometimes helps form history. At first look, it appears that luck was not kind to Lieutenant J. E. B. Stuart in the
summer of 1857 on the banks of the South Fork of the Solomon
River. He was shot in the chest. Then again, he was lucky that the
bullet didn't kill him. Though Stuart never claimed that his wounding provided him a wake-up call, it may have played a part in the
lust for life that became his trademark four years later. In account
after account, Stuart's men told how their general remained calm
despite bullets and cannonballs whizzing past him. Since he'd already experienced the pain of being shot, perhaps the fear of the
unknown no longer bothered him.

Stuart was already an old hand around Kansas in the summer
of 1857 when the government decided to move against the Cheyenne Indians in retaliation for several raids on wagon trains the
previous fall. The Cheyenne, peaceful since signing a treaty in which

they agreed to allow wagon trains to move westward without fear of attack, were puzzled when Indian agents brought them news of the impending campaign. The army ignored the treaty, which had been negotiated by a local Indian agent, rather than by any of their officers. Army leaders back in Washington determined that they had to show the Cheyenne who was in command in the Kansas Territory.

By May 1857, the army had organized an expedition commanded by Colonel Edwin Sumner. Major John Sedgwick was second in command. Both men would become generals in the Union army five years later.

Stuart rode with Sumner's column as commander of Company G of the First United States Cavalry. The campaign strategy was simple: March westward in two widely spaced columns along the northern and southern parts of the territory from Fort Leavenworth, meet at Fort Laramie (in what is now Colorado), then cut back through the center of the Cheyenne hunting grounds. The campaign would last at least two months.

In mid-July, the Cheyenne learned that the soldiers were on their way. Rather than melt away into the vast plains, they decided to fight. Two of their medicine men, Ice and Dark, assured the braves that they had developed a special technique that would render everyone who believed in it invulnerable to the firearms carried by the soldiers. Most of the Indians were armed with arrows and lances, while the cavalrymen had cap-and-ball revolvers, single-shot muzzleloading carbines, and sabers.

On July 29, Sumner finally found the Cheyenne at this site west of Morland. A West Point graduate like most of his officers, he noted that the Indians had picked out some fair defensive ground. Some 300 to 600 warriors were drawn up along the South Fork of the Solomon River. The surrounding hills both shielded their movements and broke up the advance of the cavalry. The army, trained in how to flank opposing forces, could not use that tactic here.

The Cheyenne were ready to fight, or so they thought. Dark and Ice had sold them on the idea that all they had to do to stop the rifle and pistol balls was raise their hands once the soldiers fired, and the balls would drop to the ground.

Sumner's men were ready, too. He ordered his six companies forward in three columns. As they drew closer, he had the men unsling their Sharps carbines. The Indians watched. They expected this. Both sides rode slowly toward each other. There would be no maneuvering, only a stand-up fight. The older soldiers joked with each other, teasing the nervous, younger ones that they should have eaten, as it was better to die on a full stomach.

Then Sumner did something that surprised both his men and the Cheyenne. He ordered the men to put away their carbines and draw their sabers. If the Indians were going to fight with sharp-edged weapons, so was the United States Army. The Cheyenne looked at each other and then at their medicine men. They knew that their technique could stop bullets, but there was no time to develop medicine against the soldiers' long knives. Just as the cavalry shifted from a gallop to a full charge, the Indians turned and

The location of the sod fort at the Battle of Soloman's Fork

ran. The soldiers, spoiling for a fight for more than two months, were stunned. The Cheyenne, thought to be fierce warriors, were running without having even fired an arrow in their direction.

The battle, such as it was, started in the area near the bridge and ranged several miles east. Without any regard for formation, the soldiers pursued whatever Indians they could see. This breakdown in discipline might have worked against them, had the Indians been planning a trap. Fortunately for the soldiers, the Cheyenne fled in all directions.

Stuart and two other officers chased down a single Cheyenne who was unhorsed. To their surprise, the Indian drew a pistol, a weapon not normally carried by warriors. It was an Allen revolver, a small "pepperbox" pistol normally carried by civilians, renowned for its inaccuracy and unreliability. The Allen's hammer would frequently snap down on its cylinders' percussion caps several times before the caps would ignite. Just as the Indian was about to fire on an unhorsed Lieutenant Lundsford Lomax, the mounted Stuart rushed by his friend and slashed the Indian in the thigh with his saber. (In saving Lomax, Stuart performed a valuable service for future historians. Lomax became a fair Confederate general, but his real value was in acting as editor of the *Official Records of the War of the Rebellion* and as a commissioner for Gettysburg National Military Park.) The Indian threw a shot at Stuart but missed. Another officer, Lieutenant David Stanley, then got close enough to the Indian to fire his pistol, but he, too, missed. As the Cheyenne advanced on Stanley, whose pistol was now empty, Stuart rushed up and slashed at the Indian's head with his saber. Just before he went down, the Cheyenne took aim at Stuart's chest and pulled the trigger.

Stuart seemed more surprised than injured when the bullet hit his sternum and deflected deep into his chest underneath his left nipple. The shot, probably a .22 or .25 caliber ball, did not even knock him off his horse. This indicates either that the Indian had not put enough gunpowder behind the ball or that it was old powder that had been in the pistol since loaded by its first owner, likely a settler killed by the Indians. Severely wounded by Stuart's saber slash, the Indian was finished off by Lomax and Stanley. They then got Stuart off his horse and put him in the shade of a blanket held up by sabers stuck in the ground. They sent for the surgeon, then made a stretcher for Stuart and carried him back to this spot. It was not recorded whether the surgeon removed the bullet from Stuart. Since some accounts claim that it was buried deep in his chest, it seems likely that it was left where it was.

Altogether, probably fewer than 300 soldiers engaged in the battle. Two were killed and nine wounded, including Stuart. The army claimed that eight warriors were killed, while the Indians admitted to losing four. Sumner, determined to make the Indians put up a real battle, rested only a day before setting off after them. He left one infantry company behind to protect the wounded.

The soldiers who remained in the area busied themselves by cutting and stacking sod blocks into a crude fort 50 feet square. They also built a stockade for their horses. On August 4, at least 30 Indians attacked the fort. Neither side suffered any injuries. The firing of a couple of cannon rounds frightened off the Indians.

On August 8, Stuart and the rest of the men started for Fort Kearny, more than 120 miles north in what is now Nebraska. Several days after the march began, the Pawnee scouts who supposedly knew the way abandoned the party. Stuart and a handful of men on horseback pressed ahead. They crossed swollen streams and wandered for a while before finally finding the road to Fort Kearny. They made it to safety on August 17, after which they sent soldiers back for the men on foot and those seriously wounded.

Stuart apparently did not complain about Sumner's behavior during and after the battle, but no one would have blamed him or any of the other soldiers if they had. Sumner had ordered his men to put away their long-distance carbines and switch to sabers, almost guaranteeing that they would suffer casualties when they faced the Cheyenne in face-to-face combat. He then left his wounded behind in hostile Indian territory. The Cheyenne obviously figured out that the wounded remained, as evidenced by the attack on the sod fort. Sumner also failed to assign officers or dependable Indian guides who knew the region well enough to get the wounded and the infantry back to safety. Worst of all, he did not even leave the wounded party a compass. Instead, he gave only general directions on how to find Fort Kearny. It was more luck than skill that brought the men out of the wilderness. Once, Stuart and his small party traveled in the wrong direction for more than a day when the sun was obscured by dense fog. They had to navigate the vast grass prairies using nothing more than the position of the sun.

Sumner's poor judgment did not bring any immediate punishment. Though he went on to become a Union general, he never commanded an army on his own. Stuart, a lowly lieutenant when Sumner was a full colonel in 1857, would surpass his old commander in both fame and rank in less than five years.

This incident in Stuart's life is a great subject for speculation. What if the Cheyenne had fired an arrow—rather than a small bullet from a weak revolver—point-blank into Stuart's chest? What if the revolver had been a well-made, large-caliber weapon, rather than something a gambler would conceal in his pocket? What if the wound had become infected on the plains and done more than make Stuart sore for a few days? What if luck had not been with Stuart's party and it had continued in the wrong direction and never found the mail road to Fort Kearny? All these scenarios lead to the same conclusion: Had matters developed even a bit differently, there never would have been a flamboyant character named J. E. B. Stuart commanding the Confederate cavalry.

Using aerial photographs, local historians have found a 50-by-50-foot plot matching the description of the sod fort. No tall grass grows in that square even to this day.

The two United States soldiers killed in the battle were buried in a common grave on a high hill east of the battlefield, according to reports. The hill that best matches that description is now the site of an abandoned elementary school just east of downtown Morland. Archaeologists are planning to dig at a slight depression in the schoolyard to see if they can find artifacts or the remains of the soldiers.

TEXAS

Laredo

Laredo is in southwestern Texas. I-35, US 59, and US 83 are the main access routes to the city. Camp Crawford was established on an elbow bend in the Rio Grande in 1849; it was renamed Fort McIntosh the following year. Fort McIntosh was Stuart's first real posting after graduating from West Point. Laredo Community College stands on the site of the fort today; it is located on West End Washington Street in the downtown area. No structures remain from Stuart's day, though part of the original parade ground still exists as an open field. Several structures from the late 1860s—a company storehouse, a post hospital, a quartermaster's storehouse, and a bakery—remain on the campus today.

Stuart learned one thing about himself as a young soldier: He wouldn't make a very good sailor. According to letters written home from aboard a ship as he was making his way to Texas and his first posting, he got seasick.

Stuart patrolled for Indians around Laredo, but his letters from those days make it sound like boring duty. The soldiers rarely saw Comanches, much less got the chance to fight them. One thing Stuart did accomplish while on the frontier was the growing of his famous thick, red, luxurious beard. He would keep it trimmed to mid-chest level for the rest of his life.

He was lucky that he spent just a year in Texas. In 1856, Jefferson Davis, then the United States secretary of war, pushed through the creation of the First and Second Regiments of the United States Cavalry. Stuart was transferred out of the Mounted Rifles and into the more modern First Regiment. Commanded by Colonel Edwin Sumner, the First was being formed at Jefferson Barracks, outside St. Louis, Missouri. That regiment and the Second were destined to be training units for leaders in the upcoming war. The First's lieutenant colonel was Joseph E. Johnston. Its major was John Sedgwick. One of its captains was George McClellan. Stuart was a second lieutenant.

Another reason Stuart was lucky he transferred out of Texas in 1855 was that, the following year, Jefferson Davis got a bright idea for fighting the Indians in hot, dry southwestern Texas. Figuring that horses were susceptible to heat and needed too much precious water in the desert climate, Davis imported 77 single-humped camels from North Africa. The unit assigned to test the camels was the Mounted Rifles, Stuart's old unit.

On paper, the animals looked promising; they could carry up to 800 pounds of supplies and did not need water as often as horses. But in reality, their feet were too soft for the rocky terrain. And they hated humans and every other animal they saw, often expressing their ire by spitting on whatever was within range. On top of that, the soldiers thought the camels smelled bad—which was saying a lot for men used to going a week without bathing. The army dropped the experiment after a year but kept the animals around for another decade. Some of them escaped into the desert, which led to scattered reports from terrified settlers attacked by weird-looking, smelly, humped animals.

It's good the experiment didn't work. The image of J. E. B. Stuart with his plumed hat and crimson-lined cape leading a cavalry charge from the hump of a camel just doesn't seem right.

Bibliography

"Battle of Hanover, The." *Community Profile*. 2002. http://
.www.hanoverchamber.com/profile.htm (August 25, 2002).

Blackford, W. W. *War Years with J. E. B. Stuart*. Baton Rouge: Louisiana State University Press, 1945.

Borcke, Heros von. *Memoirs of the Confederate War for Independence*. New York: Peter Smith Publishing, 1938.

Broun, Thomas L. "General R. E. Lee's War Horses, Traveler and Lucy Long." *Southern Crossroads*. Originally published in the August 10, 1886, *Richmond Dispatch*. http://www.csa-dixie.com/warhorses.htm (August, 25, 2002).

Chalfant, William V. *Cheyennes and Horse Soldiers: The 1857 Expedition and the Battle of Solomon's Fork*. Norman: University of Oklahoma Press, 1989.

"Civil War in Mercersburg." *Welcome to Mercersburg, Pennsylvania*. http://www.mercersburg.org/warmerc.htm (August 29, 2002).

Cooke, John Esten. *Wearing of the Gray: Being Personal Portraits, Scenes and Adventures of the War*. Bloomington: Indiana University Press, 1959.

Custer, George A. "The Official Report of Operations from the First

Brigade." http://pages.prodigy.net/rs.shoecraft/jah.htm (August 25, 2002).

Daihl, Samuel L. "1865: Our Johnnies Come Marching Home." http://www/iath.virginia.edu/vshadow2/KHS/pa.fr.johnny.html (August 25, 2002).

Davis, Burke. *J. E. B. Stuart:The Last Cavalier*. New York: Bonanza Books, 1957.

Durham, Robert L. "Flashing Sabers at Solomon's Fork." *Wild West* (February 2002): 38-44, 70.

"East Cavalry Field Battlefield Tour: East Cavalry Field at Gettysburg." *Friends of the National Parks: Gettysburg.* http://www.friendsofgettysburg.org/ECFG1.htm (August 25, 2002).

Freeman, Douglas Southall. *R. E. Lee: A Biography*. 4 vols. New York: Charles Scribner's Sons, 1934.

Gehris, Roy F., webmaster. "Major General David McMurtrie Gregg." *Pennsylvania Civil War Veterans.* 1998. http://www.geocities.com/Heartland/Hills/7117/GenGregg.html (August 27, 2001).

Hennessy, John. "Stuart's Revenge." 2002. http://militaryhistory.about.com/library/prm/blstuartsrevenge1.htm (August 25, 2002).

Hogue, James K. "Phillip St. George Cooke." In *American National Biography*. New York: Oxford University Press, 1999.

"J. E. B. Stuart Comes to Rockville." *Peerless Rockville.* http://members.aol.com/hilld1/ (August 25, 2002).

Johnson, Clint. *Touring Virginia's and West Virginia's Civil War Sites*. Winston-Salem, N.C.: John F. Blair, Publisher, 1999.

Longacre, Edward. *The Cavalry at Gettysburg*. Cranbury, N.J.: Associated University Press, 1986.

―――. *Mounted Raids of the Civil War*. Cranbury, N.J.: A. S. Barnes and Company, 1975.

McClellan, Henry B. *I Rode with J. E. B. Stuart: The Life and Campaigns of Major General J. E. B. Stuart*. New York: Da Capo Press, 1994.

Meserve, Steve. "Rebel Spy Story Just a Good Yarn." *Washington Times On-Line*. http://www.washtimes.com/civilwar/20020330-58204516.htm.

Mewborn, Horace. "A Wonderful Exploit: Jeb Stuart's Ride Around the Army of the Potomac." *Blue & Gray* 15 (Summer 1998): 55-65.

Perry, Tom, "Antebellum: J. E. B. Stuart in the United States Cavalry, 1854-1861." Unpublished chronological history of Stuart's United States Army career, 2002. E-mail laurelhill@jebstuart.org.

Place, Harold C. "The Civil War Began in Kansas 80 Years Ago." *Voices, the Kansas Collection Online Magazine*. 1996. http://www.kancoll.org/voices/1996/1296plac.htm (August 25, 2002).

Powell, David. "Stuart's Ride: Lee, Stuart, and the Confederate Cavalry in the Gettysburg Campaign." *Gettysburg Discussion Group*. http://www.gdg.org/stuart (August 25, 2002).

Robertson, James I., Jr. *Stonewall Jackson: The Man, the Soldier, the Legend*. New York: Macmillan, 1997.

Schuricht, Hermann. "Jenkins' Brigade in the Gettysburg Campaign: Extracts from the Diary of Lieutenant Hermann Schuricht of the Fourteenth Virginia Cavalry." *Gettysburg Discussion Group*. http://www.gdg.org/ajenkins.html (August 25, 2002).

"Soldier's Life: Camp Qui Vive, Stuart's Headquarters." *The War for States' Rights*. http://civilwar.bluegrass.net/SoldiersLife/campquivive.html (August 25, 2002).

Spring, Leverett Wilson. "Kansas: The Prelude to the War for the Union." *The Kansas Collection*. http://www.kancoll.org/books/spring/ (August 27, 2002).

Stanchak, John E. "Phillip St. George Cooke." In *Historical Times Illustrated Encyclopedia of the Civil War*. New York: Harper & Row, 1986.

Stuart, J. E. B. "The Kiowa and Comanche Campaign of 1860 As

Recorded in the Personal Diary of Lt. J. E. B. Stuart." Edited by W. Still Robinson. *Kansas Collection: The Kansas Historical Quarterly*. http://www.kancoll.org/khq/1957/57_4_robinson.htm (August 25, 2002).

Thomas, Emory M. *Bold Dragoon: The Life of J. E. B. Stuart*. New York: Harper & Row, 1986.

Trigg, George Lockwood. "Civil War Veteran John A. Huff, 1816-1864." http://pages.prodigy.net/rs.shoecraft/jah.htm (August 25, 2002).

Trout, Robert J. *They Followed the Plume: The Story of J. E. B. Stuart and His Staff*. Mechanicsburg, Pa.: Stackpole Books, 1993.

"Who Was Antonia Ford?" http://users.erols.com/kfraser/fairfax/antonia.html (August 25, 2002).

Wittenburg, Eric J. "The Approach to Brandy Station and the Grand Reviews." *Gettysburg Discussion Group*. http://www.gdg.org/brandy2.html (August 27, 2002).

Zimmerman, Daniel. "J. E. B. Stuart: Gettysburg Scapegoat?" http://militaryhistory.about.com/library/prm/blgettysburgscapegoat1.htm (August 25, 2002).

Index